# THE
# KICKASS
# COVEN

THE

# KICKASS
# COVEN

## HOW TO CREATE A WITCHY SISTERHOOD
## TO EMPOWER YOURSELF
## AND CHANGE THE WORLD

AMELIA WOOD

CASTLE POINT BOOKS

NEW YORK

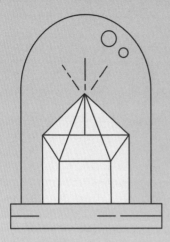

# CONTENTS

# MAGICAL ACTIVISM AND MARGARITAS

**Intrigued by the whole magical activism thing?** Ready to team up with a few like-minded witches for magic and margaritas? This book is for you. You won't find any toil and trouble here (except for the good kind). You also won't find any judgment for just dipping your toes. Embracing your inner witch to get shit done where people and politics have failed is for everyone—from old-school Wiccans to the crystal-curious—and it doesn't have to be a fucking chore.

You deserve to have a trusted circle of friends and a safe, supportive space to have fun, nurture your magic, and maybe do some good in this batshit crazy world. Lucky for you, finding a few badass witches like yourself to help you effect real change is easier and more rewarding than you've ever imagined. Whether you're a baby witch or a veteran loner, trust that you'll find what you need in *The Kickass Coven*. You were called to pick it up, weren't you?

## Who Needs a Coven?

You do. Most of us are Hermione, not Dumbledore. We need our people. With them come support, resources, knowledge, and growth. As part of a coven, you get to combine your unique experiences and strengths with those of others and perform powerful, world-changing collaborative magic. We may have all wanted that letter from Hogwarts, but the bonus of not getting one is having the opportunity to *choose* your people instead of being thrown in with the Malfoys of the magical world. You deserve sisters who bring out your best, and that's exactly what this fucked-up world of ours needs.

## Who Is This Sh*t For?

This book is for anyone who's even remotely interested in finding their people and changing the world through collaborative magic. Yes, it breaks things down for beginning witches. And yes, it's peppered with pop culture, from *Harry Potter* to the *Chilling Adventures of Sabrina*. The only requirements are a sense of humor and a high tolerance for curse words. (Actual *curses*, not so much.)

If you're more advanced or more strict in your practice, you can still get a ton of helpful information out of this book. As with all magic, you have to go into it with an open mind. Don't get stuck on "I already know that" or "That's not how I do it." Set an intention to find the information that will serve you or move the fuck on.

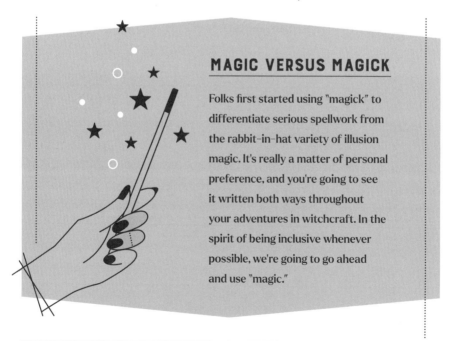

### MAGIC VERSUS MAGICK

Folks first started using "magick" to differentiate serious spellwork from the rabbit-in-hat variety of illusion magic. It's really a matter of personal preference, and you're going to see it written both ways throughout your adventures in witchcraft. In the spirit of being inclusive whenever possible, we're going to go ahead and use "magic."

## Not into Labels?

Witchcraft can be so many things, from a strict religion to a laid-back practice, a solo journey of self-discovery to a kickass sisterhood that can change the world. Your magic, your choice! The same thing goes with covens. Traditionally, a coven is a group of at least three witches who work magic together. You may also come across the term "study circle," which refers to a less experienced group of witches. But we're not going to get hung up on numbers or labels. Traditional is for other people. Your coven and your practice can be whatever the hell you want them to be.

Don't worry about the seemingly females-only vibe of witchcraft, either. Magic is for everyone, inclusive of all gender identities. Witches pull their energy from the natural world—a.k.a. Mother Earth, a.k.a. the Divine Feminine—so we're all "sisters" here. But witchcraft embraces the dichotomy of masculine and feminine in all things and favors neither.

## Modern-Day Magic DGAF

Harry Potter and his pals were obviously badass magical activists, but defeating Voldemort would have been a hell of a lot easier with a few Google searches. We're facing big, hairy, intersectional 21st-century problems, like pandemics, supercharged natural disasters, and unprecedented inequity. And we need to use all the tools available to us. There's never been a more important time to lower our wards and let witchcraft be all the things—serious, fun, simple, complex, and most of all, inclusive.

Sure, you're still going to find witches who still want to wear dark robes and chant spells that sound like Shakespearean monologues. And, to be honest, who among us has not wanted to dance naked under a full moon? But Magic knows what's up. It's ready to fight. And it doesn't give a damn whether you're using a cauldron or a hot-pink-enameled Dutch oven, whether your spells rhyme, or whether your white candle has "smells like margaritas and regret" written on the label. It only cares about intention. So let's get intentional.

## Step into Your Power

Whether you know it or not, you tap into your magic *all the damn time*. It's not out at a bar somewhere, eating peanuts and waiting for your fucking text. It doesn't need engraved invitations or flowers and romance. It's in you. All the time. Infusing every thought, word, and action. So ditch the bullshit idea that it's all dark and scary, relax, and focus on tuning into that intrinsic power of yours.

Just being around other women and feeding off each other's kickass energy is magical. Whether you delve deeper into the craft than that is your choice. Practice in whatever way feels most powerful to you. And if that involves brunch and badassery, you've come to the right place!

## Change the F*cking World

No matter which kind you practice, witchcraft is all about inclusivity, female empowerment, subversion of the status quo, environmentalism, and the impact of positive energy. Fighting the patriarchy is in our damn DNA. Harnessing the power of the natural world to effect real, positive change is What. We. Do. And *The Kickass Coven* can help you do it. Not only will it help you find your witchy sisters, it will also give you the magical tools and skills you need to make the world a better place together. Are you ready?

### WORD OF WARNING

You'll find most rituals in Part 3 of *The Kickass Coven*, but a handful are scattered throughout, where they might prove especially useful. If you're pretty new to this whole magic thing, take the time to read through the book and come back to these rituals. You might think, "Looks easy enough." And it is . . . when you know what the hell you're doing. Reading the book will be painless—delightful, even. No one can guarantee the same if you fuck with magic without having a respectful understanding of it.

# PART ONE

# FIND YOUR F*CKING PEOPLE

"Where there
is a woman,
there is magic."

—————— ❬ • ❭ ——————

NTOZAKE SHANGE

# CHAPTER 1

# START WITH YOU, BOO

**W**hen you feel like something's missing, it's pretty tempting to look for it outside of yourself. (Who wants to do all that "inner work"? Ugh.) But witchcraft is about bringing out that inner badass. The better you know yourself and what you want, the easier it is to tap into your magic, find your people, and change the fucking world. Like it or not, you've got some work to do on you. (Don't worry—you're going to like it.)

## To Thine Own Damn Self Be True

Bringing out your inner badass means you have to *go in and look for her*. Thanks to a lifetime of living with other people's expectations, not many people can really say they know who they are and what they want. You're going to need to break that shit down.

- **Grab a cocktail and some cake.** Getting to know the real you is a process—one that's often made better by libations. Treat it like a flirtatious first date. (Don't get sloppy, though. You've got shit to do.)

- **Be kind to you.** It's not your fault the world has been pushing you into a damn Popsicle mold since you were born. When you're figuring out *who* you are, do it with an appreciation for *all* you are despite that fact.

- **Take a good, hard look at yourself.** You want to get clear on your strengths, your weaknesses, your likes, your dislikes. See the whole picture. Meditate on it or just make a pro-con list, if you like that sort of thing.

### ✦ What's Working for You?

Now that you've got the breakdown, think about the aspects of your life that you like. Not the shit everyone says you should be grateful for. The shit you, personally, actually enjoy. Then throw in the stuff you like *about yourself.* Your crazy cackle, the beauty mark on your chin, how generous you are with your time, the way you eat ice cream from the bottom of the cone like a fucking weirdo— anything and everything that's uniquely you and puts a smile on your face. Bringing all of that into your magic will make it way more fucking powerful.

### ✦ What's Not?

It'll be tricky, but see if you can extract all the bullshit from this little personality profile of yours. Ditch the *shoulds* first—all those obligations, the unsolicited advice, the ways you try to fit in with someone else's idea of who you are. That shit needs to go. The *coulds* are next. If you feel guilty about something you're not doing, but you also have zero fucking interest in doing it, be done with it. Finally, think about all the crap you put *yourself* through. Not all pressure comes from outside forces. You need to let go of what you think your life is supposed to look like and embrace what it is. There's no fucking room in magic for even well-intentioned fronting. You have to be real for shit to work.

### ✦ What Do You Need to Work On?

Now that you know what makes you *you,* think about the things in your life that make you a *better* you, even if you don't like them. (Looking at you, spin class.) Write those down. Then add in all the shit you want to work on. Do you suck

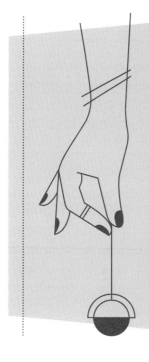

## PRACTICAL MAGIC

All this inner work can hit you right in the feels. This is where a pendulum can come in handy. (See page 84 for a full how-to.) Prime yours by asking a question to which you know the answer is Yes. Simply hold that question in your mind, hold the pendulum in your hand, and see which way it swings. That direction is Yes, and the opposite is No. Whenever you're feeling indecisive, ask the question and let your pendulum do the answering. It feeds directly off your energy so you can get out of your fucking head.

at sitting still for meditation? Meditate more. Do you feel like your knowledge of witchy history is weak? Put some books on that to-do list. Fill in as many magical gaps as you can, and your coven can help you level up instead of you just keeping up.

## Factor in the Witchy Sh*t

Once you know who you want to be as a person, you can figure out who you want to be as a witch. Are you looking for a full-time religion? Feeling more free-spirited? How do you feel about being called a witch? Find the practices and words that feel authentic to you, even if they're not conventional. Just make sure you're not avoiding things out of embarrassment or insecurity. There's no half-assing magic—not if you want it to work. You have to be all in. But you get to define the terms!

## KNOW YOUR SH'T ABOUT WICCA

Your coven can be anything you want it to be—that's the beauty of modern witchcraft. But, if you're going to fuck with magic, it's important to know the difference between witchcraft and Wicca. Wicca is its own religion, with super-specific traditions, holidays, and practices. Wiccans have had to put up with a lot of shit over the centuries, and they're not here for the appropriation all over their feeds. However you choose to practice magic, be respectful of your witchy sisters and brothers. In other words: have fun with it, but don't dick around.

## Figure Out What the Hell You Want

Covens are a messy business when you don't come at them with a plan. So you have some decisions to make before you bring other people into this shit. (If you're a Gemini, you better call someone.) Getting clear on what you want takes time, research, and a whole lot of introspection. Know what else requires those things? Practicing magic. Get used to these deep dives. They're the first step in this magical choose-your-own-adventure book. Once you know what you want, you can start working toward getting it.

### ✧ Meditate

If you want to practice magic, you better get real comfortable sitting with your-self. Light some candles, dim the lights, quiet your mind, and turn your attention inward. (Meditation takes practice, so don't be discouraged if your thoughts start pinging between what you had for breakfast last Tuesday and tomorrow's to-do list.) Focus on how you want your coven to *feel*. Not what it looks like or who's in it. Start with the vibe and the rest will fall into place.

### ✦ Visualize

Meditation clears your mind. Visualization fills it up intentionally. As in, *with intention*. So let's say you want to draw some inspiration from the *Chilling Adventures of Sabrina* (as good a place as any!). First, you meditate. Then, you visualize. That way, you can avoid going down the fucking rabbit hole about the show's nonsensical ending and instead focus on finding inspiration in the sisterhood the Spellmans created. (Hecate would make a pretty awesome patron goddess.) How you visualize is up to you. Muse, journal, draw, collage, or build—do whatever you have to do to fill in the details on your ideal coven.

## WITCH, YOU GOT THIS!

Getting your own shit together before you bring other people into it is always a good call, but it is absolutely fucking necessary when it comes to witchcraft. Like attracts like, and you don't want a coven full of whiny, indecisive, half-assed witches who are still stuck on their exes. Do what you gotta do to Bring. Up. That. Vibe!

Meditate on what you want
Fuel your body and soul
Do your fucking research
Banish any blocks
Get clear on what you want
Set healthy intentions
Step into yourself *completely*

It's totally okay to leave a little room for growth. That's what having a coven is all about. But you better be ready to bring your full fucking self to the table.

# MAGIC-BOOSTING RITUAL BATH

Bathing rituals are like the most delicious self-care Saturday, but with a mystical ripple effect you'll feel all month. Add the new moon to the mix, and you've got yourself a powerful setup for starting fresh, setting intentions, and manifesting your innermost desires.

This particular ritual harnesses the power of cleansing herbs, intuition-amplifying oils, and energy-protecting crystals to spice up your spellwork. Plus, it's really fucking relaxing. Use it to reinvigorate your magic *and* your world-weary self.

## MAGICAL MATERIALS

A bathtub or shower (see Magical Mod)

White candles

Amethyst crystals

Labradorite crystals

Dried lavender

Whole-fat milk

Frankincense essential oil

Myrrh essential oil

Sandalwood essential oil

Cleansing herb bundle

### CLEVER WITCH TIP
Kill two birds with one stone by burning essential-oil candles that have been blended for your specific intention instead of using individual oils.

### 1: Set the Scene

Light several candles, dim the lights if you can (or just turn the damn things off if you can't), and start running your bath.

### 2: Choose Your Intention

While the water runs, begin to set your intention. This one's up to you, but it can include things like fine-tuning your intuition, releasing negative shit, and stepping into your power like the badass witch you are. Whatever you choose, close your eyes and mull it over with the crystals in your hands before mindfully dropping them into the bathwater.

### 3: Prep Your Bath

Sprinkle some relaxing lavender and a healthy pour of whole milk into the water for that silky smooth skin. (Mystical shit meets self-care Saturday, remember?) And finally, add several drops of each essential oil to your bath or a nearby diffuser.

### 4: Cleanse Everything

When your bathtub is full and looking like something out of a spa brochure, grab the herb bundle. With your intention in mind, hold the herb bundle to a candle's flame until it's burning well, then blow it out. Using your hand, gently fan the smoke toward yourself so it touches as much of your body as possible. (Word of warning: be really fucking careful where you put that smoldering bundle.) Say a little prayer if you're feeling it, then cleanse the space you're in.

### 5: Finally Get in the Damn Tub

Hold your intention while you slip slowly into the tub (being careful not to bruise your foot—or anything else—on wayward crystals) and relish the feeling of the hot water on your skin. Release the mantra and use your time in the tub to relax, breathe deeply, unwind, and just fucking enjoy some magical me time.

### 6: Enjoy the New-Moon You

When you're finished, let all the negative bullshit that's been weighing you down drain away with the water. Step out of the bath totally recharged and ready to get shit done.

> **MAGICAL MOD**
>
> No bathtub? No problem. Light candles where you can see them from the shower and place your crystals under the running water. Add your lavender and a few drops of essential oils to a vacant nook or (soapless) soap dish, where the hot water can help diffuse them without washing them away. Set your intention and then hold it in your mind while you step into the stream of the water. Then let the water wash away any lingering energy blocks and just fucking enjoy!

"Because there's one thing stronger than magic: sisterhood."

ROBIN BENWAY

# CHAPTER 2

# DO THE DAMN LEGWORK

Sadly, we can't all be born with a built-in coven like the Halliwell sisters. (How lucky was it that they had a spare sister just waiting in the wings in case of any demon-related mishaps?) But, much like actors, families can create a shit-ton of drama behind the scenes. So, really, how lucky are *you* that you get to choose your witchy sisters? Getting clear on what you're looking for in a coven member can help you figure out where to look for them. Then you can put those true-crime armchair-detective skills to good use!

## Clarity Comes First

This is *your* fucking adventure, so you get to choose your traveling companions. Consider what you want in a coven mate *as well as what you need*. You're not just looking for coffee buddies here. What qualities do your fellow witches need to have for your coven to be what you want it to be and to do what you need it to do? Let's say you want to change the world but prefer to stay behind the scenes. Then you need someone who's not afraid to be seen. Not sure where to start? Meditate, visualize, and feel those feelings.

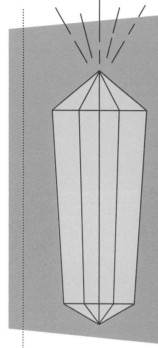

## CRYSTAL F'CKING CLEAR

When you want to get crystal fucking clear about things, reach for clear quartz crystal. Meditating with one in hand for just a minute can help you home in on the answers you seek. This stone can also help you raise your vibration, which is pretty fucking handy when you're trying to change the world. Visualize your negative vibes being cleared out by a bright, white light while you hold the crystal. With all the bullshit gone, you'll be able to see things more clearly and be more decisive about what you want.

# Search IRL

For some people, putting themselves out there is going to be the hardest part of this whole journey. (And if you're old enough to have watched the original version of *Charmed* when it aired, meeting people probably ain't as easy as it used to be.) Starting in the physical world with a six-degrees-of-you approach can help. You'd be surprised how many people you're already energetically connected to in your everyday life. By paying as much attention to your intuition as you do your checklist, you can start to spot a good fit at a fucking glance.

### ✧ Start with Your Phone

This doesn't have to be complicated. Who do you already know who would be a good fit for a kickass coven like yours? You've been unconsciously calling like-minded people into your life for the length of it, so you probably have a friend or two with an instant in. But you might find a few more possibilities in your contacts list. Remember when that one friend mentioned seeing a palm reader? That's the sign of an open mind! Set up a coffee date to feel things out.

### ✦ Think Like You

If you want people in your coven to vibe, then look for people doing shit you like to do. Where do you spend your time? Start there. Most of us have a "get in, get out" mentality when we go places without friends in tow. Instead of keeping your head down, pick it the fuck up. Look around and notice people and their energy. It might go against everything in your "Who the fuck calls people anymore??" nature, but *talk* to people. It (probably) won't kill you.

### ✦ Expand the Search

Sure, not *every* witch is a reiki instructor by day. But being a reiki instructor definitely increases your odds of having dabbled in witchcraft. It just does. No one wants to stereotype here, but certain places and practices lend themselves to the sort of open mind that magic requires. Keep an eye out for holistic healers,

## PRACTICAL MAGIC

Break out that trusty pendulum again! This time, you're going to try dowsing (divining) for friendship. Grab a map of your area. If you don't have a physical map, sketch one out with a few landmarks dropped in. (It doesn't have to be fucking art—it just has to get the job done.) Then hold your pendulum over the map, close your eyes, and charge it with your intention (e.g., to find people who would be an awesome fucking fit for your coven). Drag a finger over the map while keeping an eye on your pendulum. Stop wherever it signals Yes, then make a note to check that place out!

yoga teachers, entrepreneurs, artists, and environmentalists. Take a yoga or meditation class. Hang out in the "New Age" section of the bookstore. Sign up for a moonlit hike. There's bound to be a reiki master or two who also likes unicorn lattes and smashing the patriarchy.

# Find Your People Online

For witches with social anxiety—or just a general disdain for humanity—searching for potential coven members online might be the way to go. There's no Bumble BFF for witches (although that should absolutely be a thing). But there are still plenty of ways to find your witches online—including apps like Bumble BFF. Just keep in mind that the Internet can be an even scarier place than a Bikram yoga studio on a commune with no running water. Proceed with caution.

### ✦ Be a Follower (Just This Once)

As a badass magical activist, one of the only acceptable times to be a follower is when you're following someone amazing on social media. But leave the influencers for another time, like when you need some altar inspo. You're looking for local people who share your interests and seem open to your particular style of witchery. Notice people who seem comfortable expressing their whole selves online—this makes it easier to know if they'll fit in with your coven's vibe. Since this is nearly fucking impossible to know from a carefully curated profile, follow, lurk, comment, form a relationship, *then* DM. The important part is the lurking. See what the person posts and how they interact with people before you invest too much time or energy into connecting with them.

### ✦ Set Some F*cking Boundaries

Searching online may seem like an easy option, but keep in mind that the interwebs can be a black hole of crazy. You're going to have to put up some protective wards, both physically and energetically. Stick with popular sites and skip the fringey forums that look like they never made it past 1998. And be super fucking selective about who you reach out to directly. No matter how excited you are about the idea

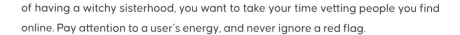

of having a witchy sisterhood, you want to take your time vetting people you find online. Pay attention to a user's energy, and never ignore a red flag.

### ✦ Avoid Virtual Pitfalls

We all live our lives online now, so you're probably painfully aware of the pitfalls from a text-conversation-gone-wrong situation of your own. Just remember that these people don't know you either. For all they know, you're one of the black-hole people. So be mindful about how you present yourself, adjusting for their inability to read your face or hear your tone. Once you're mutually assured of the other's relative sanity, you can move on to video chat.

And, above all, remember that online is forever. Even the best intentions can get twisted, so watch what you post. You don't want some crazy witch making voodoo dolls of you.

## WITCH, YOU GOT THIS!

Finding witches you like and want to hang with is no easier than making friends. But the good news is, it's no harder, either. We're all people first. And whether they know it or not, your future coven mates are looking for you, too.

Get clear on what you want in a sister

Get clear on what your coven needs in a member

Consider who you already know

Just fucking talk to people

Find the good on social media

Protect your energy from crazies

Cautious optimism is the name of this game. You're just keeping your mind and your options open at this point. The deep dive comes next!

# A RECIPE
## FOR FRIENDSHIP

Look, making friends can be hard. Making friends who are into magic and brunch and saving the world but not into hexing their shitty bosses? Harder. Luckily, like attracts like—especially where magic's involved.

Of course, you can always give that natural magic a little boost with some of the intentional kind. This ritual helps you break through any lingering energetic barriers you may have to finding new friends (and coven members) while also helping you attract badass witches like yourself. Put your own spin on it with crystals, candles, incense, and items that speak to the virtues you value.

## MAGICAL MATERIALS

A white candle

Matches or lighter

Pen

Paper

Envelope

Crystals like yellow topaz (for joy), rose
    quartz (for compassion), or lapis lazuli
    (for communication)

Scents like honey (sweetness), cinnamon
    (spice), or lavender (calm)

### CLEVER WITCH TIP
Don't be afraid to use non-magical items in your spellwork. As long as they mean something to you, they infuse the spell with your intention.

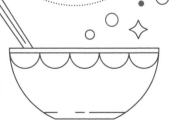

### 1: Get Ready for Bed

You can perform this ritual anytime, but doing it during the new moon lets you tap into its manifestation magic. Start preparing for it at night, shortly before you're ready to go to bed.

### 2: Prepare Your Space

Hold your intention in your mind while you place your candles, crystals, incense, and whatever the hell else in a circle around the white candle. Light the white candle first, then any other candles or incense. Breathe in any scents you're using while you turn inward.

### 3: Think about What You Want

Take a few minutes to fill your thoughts with the qualities you hope for in a friend or coven mate. Supportive? Creative? Ready to change the fucking world? Sure. But don't be afraid to get weirdly specific, too—like someone who puts mustard on their French fries, if that's what's missing from your life.

### 4: Think about What You Have

Next, think about what you bring to the table. Consider all the things you love and appreciate about yourself and fill yourself with gratitude for them. These are the things you would want a friend to appreciate about you. (If you struggle with this part, you need to revel in your fucking awesomeness more often!)

### 5: Put Out the Call

Boil your intention down to a phrase. Something like, "I call into my life like minds, good vibes, and a coven that makes the world and myself better" will do the trick because you're going to infuse it with the energy you've just conjured up. Fill yourself with gratitude while you write the intention on the paper.

### 6: Seal It and Sleep on It

Say the intention out loud as you fold the paper and place it in your envelope, then use the white candle to drip some wax onto it and seal your intention. Tuck the envelope under your pillow and let it infuse your dreams. Starting the next day, carry the envelope with you to act as an energetic beacon to all around you who fit the bill.

**MAGICAL MOD**

Don't think in terms of what you *don't* want in your friendships. That will only bring more of it. If you think you'll have a hard time keeping things positive, make a list *before* starting the ritual. Divide a piece of paper into two columns: "Don't Want" and "Want." In the first column, list all the shitty things you've put up with in the past. In the other, put a positive spin on them. "Never there for me when I need them" becomes "Always there for me when I need them."

"There's a little witch in all of us."

——— ( • ) ———

ALICE HOFFMAN

CHAPTER 3

# FEEL IT OUT

Y ou've got some prospects. You're feeling things out. You've gradu-
ated from small talk to real talk. All good stuff. But telling someone
that 1) You're a witch, 2) You want to start a coven, and 3) You want
that coven to be full of badass magical activists? That's a lot. There's
no harm in keeping things low-key and working up to an invite. If they're not into
it, you avoid spooking them. If they are, you ensure they're the right fit for your
coven. Don't worry about the delay—just focus on upping your own magical
game in the meantime.

## Have Some F*cking Chill

People may seem really open-minded right up until the moment you mention
using moon water to cook your pasta. Ease into spiritual conversations. Keep
things vague at first to avoid the crazies, bullies, and people who will look at
you like you just sprouted tentacles from your ears. Once you've pushed past
the bullshit and bluster to really get to know who is on your team, *then* you can
mention the coven. Use that intuition of yours to get a feel for what others are
comfortable discussing. Not everyone is going to be into magic, and that's fine.
You might have a ton of other things in common.

## Keep It Casual

You and your witchy sisters are going to be spending a lot of time together. And if you do this right, not all of that time will be spent sweating over a cauldron or holding protest signs. For this thing to last a lifetime (or two), you need to know you enjoy each other's company. Saying that you both like yoga is one thing. Actually twisting yourselves into pretzels together is going to separate the adults

from the kids. It doesn't matter whether you both end up being yoga masters, you both suck at it, or you're at completely different levels. It only matters whether you enjoy doing it together. So take this new friendship out for a few test drives.

### ✦ Do Them

Obviously, you'll ask your potential coven mate to do something they enjoy doing first. Not only does seeing them in their element give you a sense of who they are, but also this type of courtesy shows them you weren't raised by fucking wolves. (That's important in any friendship.) No matter what they suggest, give it a try.

### CRYSTAL F'CKING CLEAR

Crystals can come in super handy, both to amplify an intention and to simply impart their own magic. Amethyst is a great one to have around when testing the waters with new people. It can protect you from negative energy, relieve social anxiety, and recharge your batteries. Hold an amethyst crystal in each palm, the right one facing out and the left one facing in. (Swap these if you're left-handed.) Visualize a circuit flowing in through the left and out through the right, filling you up with positive, revitalizing energy.

One of the major advantages of having a coven is being exposed to the different skills and perspectives that round it out and make you all better witches. But if they invite you to go mini golfing and you're a fucking pro, don't hold back on that windmill shot. It's important to see whether your new friend can be a supportive teammate in the circle.

### ✦ Do You

Next, see if they're open to the things that make you *you*. Invite them to your second-favorite coffee shop. (In case things go south. Just saying.) Gauge their openness to activism by mentioning your volunteer work or that letter-writing campaign you joined before the last election. If they don't have much experience, try to find out whether they're excited to get involved in the future. You can also try to work your favorite witchy books and movies into the conversation to test a person's openness to magic. If you wear a "Sanderson Sisters' Inn" tee shirt to brunch and they ask if you liked staying there, this thing wasn't going to work out anyway.

### ✦ Try Something New

Magical activism isn't for the faint of heart. Your work in both the circle and the world is going to throw shit at you that you never saw coming. It's important to know that you and the other members of your coven can handle it. One of the best ways to suss that out early? Do something neither one of you has ever done before. Try that new Mexican place. Hop a plane to actual Mexico. Do whatever calls to you both. If you can handle the unknown together, you're already better off.

## Get Curious

Following your curiosity is another way of honoring your intuition—it's your subconscious telling you "This is what you need to know." (Unless you're a Gemini and it's just your relentless need to know everything.) Take a genuine interest in your potential coven mate. Ask questions, but more importantly, really listen when the other person speaks. Feel their words washing over you. This is about

## PRACTICAL MAGIC

Your intuition is more than just your internal compass—it's a psychic muscle you need to exercise. Lucky for you, that's a hell of a lot easier and more enjoyable to do than riding a stationary bike. It starts with a daily meditation ritual. Don't roll your eyes. All you need is 5 fucking minutes a day. By learning to quiet your own thoughts, you can hear your intuition whispering to you, guiding you. You'll know it's your intuition speaking, and not your anxiety or your ego, when you feel completely relaxed and grounded.

more than just being a good friend. (That's obviously pretty fucking important, too, though.) It's about tapping into your magical spidey sense.

### ✦ Vibe Check

In the magical world, vibe checks are about more than just making sure your girls are having a good time. (OK, yes, sometimes it's about that.) Being attuned to the energy of the people around you is one of a witch's most valuable skills, and all it takes is a little practice—and a little multitasking. While you're with someone, check in with how you're feeling. Invigorated? Loving? Inexplicably drained? Sinking into the pit that's suddenly developed in your stomach? If you can't attribute those feelings to something else, like the waiter calling you "ma'am," pay fucking attention to them. But also pay attention to what they're saying so you don't look like a dick.

### ✦ Eyes Open

Frankly, we're all a bunch of judgy bitches. There's no getting around it. So we should absolutely practice looking for the good in people. You don't throw away a potentially amazing friend just because she has garbage taste in men and burritos. But looking for the good doesn't mean ignoring the bad. There's no place for rose-colored glasses when you're looking at a potential coven mate. Magic doesn't change us—it amplifies who we are. So, notice your new friend's habits and ask yourself whether you'd mind them with some magic behind them.

## Be Picky

You're the average of the five people you hang out with, so make sure everyone adds to the damn equation. Not everyone is coven worthy, and that's OK. It doesn't mean you have to ghost them. But you don't have to feel guilty about not extending an invite to everyone whose company you enjoy. And you definitely don't have to think twice about (politely) showing a bad fit the door. This is your coven, and you have big fucking plans for it. Start with a crew who gets it and go from there.

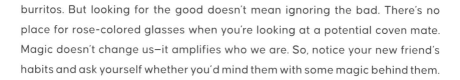

## WITCH, YOU GOT THIS!

Sure, you're excited to get to the magical badassery. But you can't bust out the pentagrams and protest signs your first time out with a new friend.

Keep the coven shit quiet for now
Spend some time together
Be open to new things
Drop some (very subtle) witchy hints
Pay attention to how you feel
Don't overlook bad habits
Hold out for the ones who get it

Getting to know people before you drop magic into the convo helps you avoid the crazies and ensures you don't look like one to others. That's all upside.

"A witch is just
a girl who knows
her mind."

— ( • ) —

CATHERYNNE M. VALENTE

# CHAPTER 4

# CHOOSE THE REAL ONES

**F**irst and foremost, a coven should be a place of trust, respect, love, support, and friendship. Having that kind of solid foundation in place is the only way your magic is going to work. And although liking your coven mates is a huge part of that, it's just one part. Equally important is that each member contributes to your vision for the coven. You're the ringmaster of this circus. Do you want incredible performers? Or do you want Side-show Bob (murderous impulses and all)? That's why you do your due diligence before you extend an official invite.

## Make Sure They Get It

Finding the right fit for your coven takes work. Do the thing right, and a new friend can become your witchy sister for life. Do it wrong, and, well.... Best case scenario, you've got some hurt feelings. Worst case, you're the proud new owner of a restraining order and you can't go to your favorite coffee shop anymore. (Hey, you were warned.) You don't always know a bad seed when you do yoga with one. And not every awesome person is right for *your* coven. But by looking at things with your intention in mind and your intuition on tap, you can make sure you find the right fit.

### ✧ Know Your Deal Breakers

Remember when we talked about *not* being a judgy bitch? That doesn't apply to deal breakers. These are the things that make you want to scream into a pillow (or at a driver who doesn't use a damn turn signal). The bottom line is, this is your fucking coven. If you don't like people who slurp their coffee, then you don't invite people who slurp their coffee. You can't harness your magic when you're annoyed as fuck. And this probably goes without saying, but consider some age limits. You probably don't want a casting-curious sixteen-year-old in your group of twenty-somethings.

### ✧ Have the Talk

If you haven't had the conversation yet, it's time. You don't have to mention the coven right away. Start with, "I'm really into this idea of magical activism" and go from there. Let them lead the conversation so you can gauge their interest. Answer any questions they might have about what it is. As long as things go smoothly, you can bring up the concept of a coven. Again, skip the specifics until they stop making that "wtf is she even talking about" face. And don't give the invite until they pass the test (keep reading).

### ✧ Make Sure You're on the Same Damn Page

This is a big one when it comes to coven members: being on the same page about what kind of witchcraft you want to practice. If you want to perform healing rituals on developing nations in crisis while your witchy sister wants to hex ex-boyfriends, she's probably not a good fit. (Say it with me: we do not hex people. Even when they suck.) Ask yourself if potential members are down with your activist ambitions. There are plenty of covens that focus on personal shit. But if you want yours to be full of badass witchy warriors for good, you need to know the others are into it.

## KNOW YOUR SH'T ABOUT THE RULE OF THREE

One thing that witches of all stripes generally agree on is the Rule of Three (a.k.a. The Threefold Law or the Law of Return). Basically, it's the idea that whatever energy, magic, or action you put out into the world comes back to you—times three. So don't fuck with dark magic, negative vibes, or bad witches unless you want that stuff knocking on your door in a big way.

## See If They Pass the Test

If you're type A (or a Capricorn) and got really excited about making people pass an actual exam to get into your coven, settle down. This isn't that kind of test. We're going to call this the "Golden Girls" test. Summon the magic of Blanche Devereaux (if anyone's a witch, she was) to find the ultimate companions. Or just use this handy checklist:

- Do you like them?
- Can you be fully yourself around them?
- Can you learn from them?
- Are they open to learning from others?
- Is their energy invigorating (not draining)?
- Are they open to magic?
- Are they cool with your rules?
- Will they lend you their good earrings?
- Will they eat copious amounts of cheesecake with you?

Those last two are especially important, obviously. If you answered Yes to these questions—or at least to the ones that matter to you—then you're good to go!

## CRYSTAL F*CKING CLEAR

A combo of lapis lazuli, moss agate, and rose quartz can encourage and support friendship, bring balance, and help you forge connections, not to mention amplify your own positive personality traits. And who couldn't use some good PR? Charge the stones with your intention (hold them and meditate on finding some decent fucking friends), then keep them on you until your intention is fulfilled (you find some decent fucking friends). If you feel strange having a bunch of rocks in your pocket, you can find some lovely gemstone jewelry online that'll serve the same purpose.

## Extend the Invite (Or Not)

By now, you should have at least hinted to your new friends that you're interested in magical activism. When you're sure—like, really fucking sure—about who you want in your witchy corner, it's time to let them in on the plan. Kicking someone out of a coven can get pretty awkward, so you want to be sure. That said, don't be afraid to follow your gut when inviting someone into the fold. As long as you've done the work, the chance that they'll set anything on fire is *very* small.

### ✦ When It's a Yes

You don't need to send anyone engraved invitations, but you can't just casually tell them to bring the tequila *and a cauldron* to movie night, either. By now, they should pretty much know what's up. Hopefully, they've expressed some interest in being part of it. If not, you need to let them know what they'd be getting themselves into. Be up front about what you're looking for, how they fit in, and why you want them. (A little flattery couldn't hurt here.) And make it clear that they won't be signing any contracts in blood. If you guys try it out and it doesn't work, no harm, no foul.

### ✦ When It's a No

There's no shame in someone not making the cut, whether it's a friend or some witch you found on the Internet. The coven should be a good fit for everyone. And a No right now is not necessarily a No forever. Just be sure to tread carefully when it comes to witches whose practice runs a little darker than your own. Remember—it's just about fit. Disparaging the wrong person's craft could earn you a hex. But as long as you didn't get anyone's hopes up, there's no need to even talk about the coven. In fact, what coven?

## WITCH, YOU GOT THIS!

Once you've found some good prospects, it's time to feel them out for coven life. Great friends don't always make great coven mates, and there's nothing wrong with that. You just need to know how to differentiate between the two.

............

Set some firm boundaries
Make sure everyone's working toward the same goal
See if they check all your boxes
Just say No to dark magic
Consider reciprocity in all you do
Extend invites to your top choices
Let the others down easy

............

Now that you've found your magical quorum, you can finally start to get your shit together as a coven and make a difference. Like anyone who works together (and plays together), you'll have some things to iron out. But you've already done a hell of a lot of the hard work.

"Being a witch means living in this world consciously, powerfully, and unapologetically."

GABRIELA HERSTIK

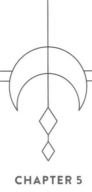

# CHAPTER 5

# CULTIVATE YOUR COVEN'S VIBE

S orry, Virgos, we're going to worry about the details a little later. (Chill— we'll get there.) Right now, you need to focus on what you want your coven to *feel* like. Tending to your emotions first will not only help you tap into your natural magic, it will also help you decide on the most logical framework for your needs. As soon as you have a rough idea, you can bring the others on board. This might be your brainchild, but you need everyone to be on the same page from the jump if it's going to fucking work.

## Raise That Vibration

If you're reading this book, then it's pretty damn clear you're not here for the fire-and-brimstone treatment. Ideally, your coven would exist somewhere in the same sphere as a book club—a place for learning and support. Is it a book club with tea? A book club with cheese? A book club with tequila, burgers, and dancing? That's up to you. But magic feeds off you, your intention, your anxiety, your emotions. So you have to keep the vibe high, and not just in terms of fun-loving positivity. You have to raise up your respect for Magic, the laws of the Universe, and your fellow witches, too.

### ✧ Keep It Low Key

The challenges you face (we all face) are demanding enough without you going all Dolores Umbridge. You can have organization without the "I will have *order*" attitude. Channel the aunts from *Practical Magic* instead: take magic seriously, but don't take yourself too seriously. And make time for margaritas. A fun, loving, supportive, and *flexible* coven is going to be way more fucking productive than one that's set in its stodgy ways. Make sure there's as much play as there is work and enough light to combat all the darkness you'll be up against as magical activists.

### ✧ Be F*cking Supportive

You've read it a few times now, but this whole "support" thing is really fucking important. No matter how much you have in common, you're all very different people. You have different tastes, different life experiences, different abilities. You can't tear each other down for any of it and still make world-changing magic together. Allow everyone to take their own journey at their own pace and be quick to forgive the occasional mistake. You're all here to learn and grow and make the world a better place. And without the support of your sisters, you're not going to get very far.

## CRYSTAL F*CKING CLEAR

Infuse your initial coven-building talks with a little easy magic from crystals that were made for the job. Citrine can bring you sunny vibes, clear quartz attracts positivity, and amethyst creates a space of light and love. You can place any or all of these stones in the center of your circle. (Or on the table at the diner. Whatever.) Take a moment to feel their energy fill you up while you set your intention to have a healthy, productive, and—dare you dream it— enjoyable time creating this kickass coven from scratch.

## Know (Roughly) What You Want

Now that you know how you want the coven to feel (e.g., supportive, fun, a little like Spring Break in Cabo), you can start to imagine its structure. We're still not worrying about the details. We're just daydreaming here (a.k.a. setting our intentions). So ponder these questions over a fruity beverage:

- Will your framework be somewhat strict or pretty flexible?
- Will you incorporate astrology? Tarot? Nordic runes? What else?
- Will you stick to certain types of magic? Or will you be open to anything?
- Will you meet in one place or bop around?

Keep pondering (and sipping) until you have a clear picture in your head of a regular Tuesday with the crew. Again, you want to be super clear before you bring other people into your vision. You'll want to ask for your coven mates' opinions, but it's helpful to know where your boundaries are before you do.

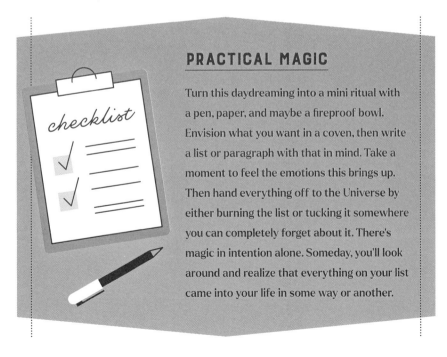

### PRACTICAL MAGIC

Turn this daydreaming into a mini ritual with a pen, paper, and maybe a fireproof bowl. Envision what you want in a coven, then write a list or paragraph with that in mind. Take a moment to feel the emotions this brings up. Then hand everything off to the Universe by either burning the list or tucking it somewhere you can completely forget about it. There's magic in intention alone. Someday, you'll look around and realize that everything on your list came into your life in some way or another.

# Have Some F*cking Respect

Yes, magic is everywhere. Yes, anyone can tap into it. And yes, you get to make up a lot of the rules as you go because magic is pretty chill overall. But disrespect Magic—with a capital M—and it'll leave you on your ass. Disrespect your sisters, and they might just do worse. Blowing off steam, taking a more lighthearted approach, and letting your personalities shine are all well and good. Just don't take that shit too far.

### ✦ For the History

Take another lesson from the Aunts—Magic does not fuck with people who look down their noses at it. This shit has been around since the dawn of time. It was here before you, it'll be here after you, and it doesn't give a damn. This book gives you an overview of magical principles, but it's worth doing some research on the history of magic and coming to understand some of the rules that more strict observers live by. Having this sort of background can help you know where to draw the line on, say, Magic and Margarita Mondays. Should you enjoy your-selves? Of course. Your joy feeds your magic. Should you be drunk when you work a spell? Absolutely not. Not only could you accidentally set your fucking shirt on fire, you could also piss off Magic and lose your witchy privileges.

### ✦ For the People

Respecting your sisters is about more than just not being a dick. It's also about hearing each other out, holding space for one another, and helping each other up when someone falls. Look, you don't know what you don't know. Everyone's coming into this with their own experiences and points of view, and they're all valid. Skip the unhelpful criticism and just try to be a decent fucking human when you disagree. Seek out, acknowledge, and focus on your sisters' strengths. And if they ask—only if they ask—try to help them with their weaknesses. In other words, treat people how you'd want to be treated. (Hmm . . . isn't that the basic idea behind the Rule of Three? Magic always comes full circle!)

### ✦ For Yourself

You're not a kid dressing up as Winifred Sanderson for Halloween anymore. And if you've read this far, you're probably not just here for the pretty crystals. This isn't playtime. (Even if you're now an adult dressing up as Winifred Sanderson for Halloween and have yet another crystal deity in your shopping cart.) You are a badass magical activist. Fucking act like it. Respect yourself enough to take your magical prowess seriously, respect your time with your sisters, and respect the work you'll do together.

# Ditch the Sh*tty Energy

If you're going to keep that vibe high, you're going to need to identify and clear out the low-vibe shit, like toxic people and energy blocks. Their source isn't always as obvious as you might think, so it's good to keep your intuition open and take note of any shifts in energy you feel throughout your days and weeks with the coven. You'll also need to take a good, hard look at yourself once in a while and make sure your magic is above-board. It's a slippery fucking slope from banishing a shitty politician to binding one (but more on that later).

### ✦ People Who Bring You Down

Don't hesitate to cleanse your coven of people who bring down your vibe. No amount of crystals or healing herbs can protect your energy when you have someone constantly bringing it down. Once you've identified the problem, take care of it. You'll find a cord-cutting ritual at the end of this chapter that's super handy for dealing with toxic assholes. Then, when they're out of your living room and life for good, make sure you do a dedicated cleansing of any space where their energy might linger.

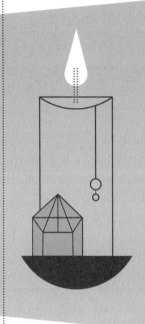

# PRACTICAL MAGIC

When you need just a light cleansing of the coven and the physical space, grab a white candle and a piece of rose quartz for each witch. Light the candle, come together in a circle around it, and hold the crystals between your clasped hands. Send up a simple prayer (together or silently) that the coven be cleansed of, and protected against, any negative energy. That's it! Think of this like the daily shower spray of cleansing rituals. This quick hit won't replace a serious cleansing for toxic energy, but it can keep the place feeling brighter in between deep cleanings.

### ✦ Badass-Energy Blockers

Stagnant spellwork and stuffy covens aren't always about toxic people bringing their bad energy. Sometimes the good shit just gets stuck somewhere, blocking up the flow. Luckily, cleansing rituals work as well for energy blocks as they do for taking out the trash. Just remember that whenever you remove bad energy or clear a block, you need to fill that void with something positive. You can visualize filling the space with white light, or you can just put on some music that makes you feel good and dance it out. (No, seriously.)

### ✦ Your Own Bullsh*t

Low vibrations can come from anyone—even you. If you feel the block is internal, close your eyes and see bright, white light slowly moving through your body from head to toe. Does it stop anywhere? You might be able to clear it out by pushing the energy through, but sometimes it's a sign of physical, mental, or emotional shit you need to deal with. Remember, magic only amplifies what's already there. When you're at your best, your magic reflects that. When you hate your job and want to throw your shoes at the wall, your magic will reflect that, too. You have to change your situation or find a healthy outlet for those emotions.

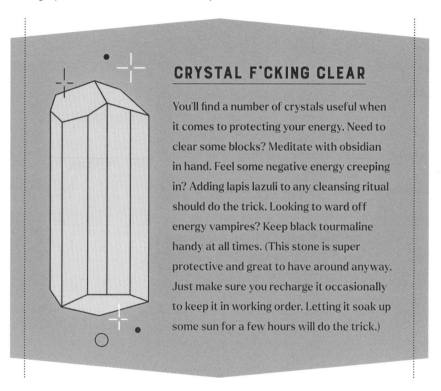

## CRYSTAL F*CKING CLEAR

You'll find a number of crystals useful when it comes to protecting your energy. Need to clear some blocks? Meditate with obsidian in hand. Feel some negative energy creeping in? Adding lapis lazuli to any cleansing ritual should do the trick. Looking to ward off energy vampires? Keep black tourmaline handy at all times. (This stone is super protective and great to have around anyway. Just make sure you recharge it occasionally to keep it in working order. Letting it soak up some sun for a few hours will do the trick.)

### ✦ Judgy Nonbelievers

This is where the detective work comes in. You can't tell a nonbeliever just by looking at them. Sometimes, they don't even realize that they're struggling with their own magic. Sometimes, they're just manipulative dicks who thought it would be fun to worm their way into your coven. And sometimes, it's the nonbelief of their family, partner, or friends rubbing off on them. Nonbelievers will bring down your vibe every time. If you find that one of your invitees was all talk, refer back to that cord-cutting ritual. If your coven mate is knee-deep in negative energy from people around them, they have some solo work to do before bringing that shit into your group.

### ✦ Dark Magic F*ckery

Remember the Rule of Three? Don't do anything to anyone that you wouldn't want boomeranging back to your ass. Even the most serious Wiccans don't believe in fucking with dark magic. (In fact, Wiccan traditions most closely resemble those of Buddhism or Hinduism, not the scary shit you see in movies.) Witchcraft is about respecting the Universe and all the living things in it. So, no adding eye of newt to your cauldron and no fucking with anyone's free will. If you put negative shit out into the world, you can't complain when you're surrounded by negative shit.

## WITCH, YOU GOT THIS!

A coven is clearly more than its rules and rituals. It's a collective of ideas and energy that feeds off love and respect. That means that, if it's going to be effective, you need to work on the emotional side of things first.

Start with how you want to feel

Skip the fire and brimstone

Have each other's backs

Set your intentions for your coven

Treat Magic with respect

Clean house of any toxic nonsense

Be a good fucking human

Magic is pretty damn flexible for being an eternal, all-powerful, life-altering entity, but it won't stand for any toxic bullshit or disrespect. Stay humble and keep those vibrations high as you turn your daydream into a reality.

# BYE, B*TCH
# CORD-CUTTING RITUAL

Hear that? That's the sound of you cutting toxic bullshit out of your life! Snip, snip, witches! Cord cutting is exactly what it sounds like—the age-old witchy art of severing energetic ties. This ritual is white-witch approved because it doesn't wish any harm on the other person. It simply finishes the job of getting them the fuck out of your life.

Rituals like this are most often used after a bad breakup (so keep it handy!), but you can adapt it for cutting out all sorts of negativity and bullshit. If you accidentally invite a bad apple into your bunch (hey, it happens), this cord-cutter will help you get the bitter taste out of your mouth.

## MAGICAL MATERIALS

Cleansing herb bundle

Florida water

Black cotton cord

A black candle

Scissors

Cauldron or fireproof bowl

### CLEVER WITCH TIP
Get creative with this ritual. It can just as easily help you cut ties with bad habits and fears that are holding you back. Just don't tie yourself too tightly so that you're stuck waiting for the delivery guy to save you.

### 1: Clear the Air

Start wherever the bad apple spent the most time fermenting—so, probably your covenstead. If that's inside, open as many windows and doors as possible. (That toxic energy has to have somewhere to go.) Light your bundle, let it burn for a few seconds, then blow it out and get that good, negativity-clearing smoke going. Then waft that shit around. Have someone spray the Florida water around the space, too.

### 2: Set Your Intentions

Light the candle and get clear about exactly what it is you want to release—in this case, a former coven member and their bullshit. Make sure everyone's on the same page if you're doing this ritual together.

### 3: Bind Your Feet

Use the cord to tie up your feet while saying, "This is the toxic garbage that keeps us from moving forward." (Or something like that—your magic, your choice.) Just don't cut off your circulation in the process.

### 4: Bind Your Wrists

Tie up your hands while saying, "This is what keeps us from getting shit done." Keep the bindings loose or you'll need to cut each other out of them like hostages in a fucking spy thriller.

### 5: Release Yourself

Sit in the bindings for a minute, visualizing them absorbing all of the toxic bullshit and negativity that surrounds you, your coven, your space, and your goals. When you're ready, use the scissors to cut those radioactive bastards off, saying something like, "We release these toxic ties and move forward feeling free and fucking powerful."

### 6: Seal in That Awesome Energy

Spritz yourselves with the Florida water to seal in the good vibes, then take a match (or lighter) to the cord cuttings in your fireproof bowl. Bury the ashes as far away from your newly cleansed space as you can without breaking any laws or pissing anyone off, and you're done!

> ### MAGICAL MOD
>
> Thinking *WTF is Florida water*? It's America's answer to Eau de Cologne, and it's chock fucking full of essential oils that make quick work of cleansing. If you don't have time to wait for two-day shipping, whip some up yourself by mixing vodka and rose water together in a spray bottle with a few drops each of lavender, lemon, orange, bergamot, cinnamon, and clove essential oils. Use your witchy intuition (and your sense of smell) to guide you on the ratios. Let it steep overnight, and *voila*!

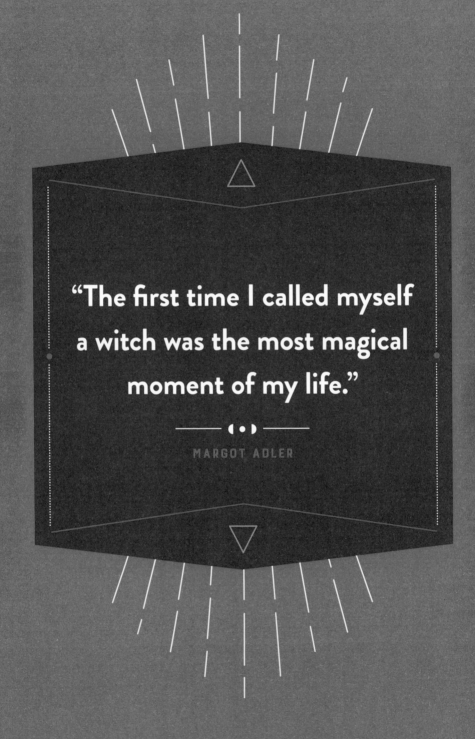

"The first time I called myself a witch was the most magical moment of my life."

MARGOT ADLER

# CHAPTER 6

# PRIORITIZE BONDING TIME

**Y**ou've found your people. You've set your intentions. You've raised your vibration. So what's next? Learning how to make magic together! You can't just throw a bunch of boys in a band and expect them to be BTS. They have to learn how to harmonize, right? The whole point of being in a coven is to harness the collective power of multiple witches, with all their unique experiences and talents. You can't do that if everyone stays in their own fucking bubble. You have to learn how to fuse and amplify that energy. Lucky for you, that's as simple as spending time together—with a few magical modifications.

## GTF Outside

Not a fan of nature? You might want to rethink this whole "witch" thing. Our energy comes from the natural world. The moon, crystals, the four elements—magic is fucking steeped in it. Some witches go so far as to worship it. So it makes perfect sense that you should spend some time in it. You can hike up a mountain, go skinny dipping under a full moon, bring a charcuterie board to the park—whatever strikes your fucking fancy! Just get outside and start to attune yourselves to nature's energy. You're going to need that connection when you dig into spellwork and rituals.

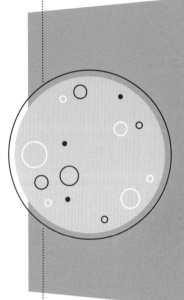

## PRACTICAL MAGIC

If you do nothing else, spend an evening under the stars, preferably on a night with a full moon. You can be sitting around a firepit and sipping rosé if you want to. No judgment here. But spend some time letting the moon's light wash over you. Feel it charging up your energy stores. You're going to tap into this magic often for your rituals, using the moon's phases to amplify your intentions and manifest your greatest desires. Start to develop a relationship with it early on and as a group.

## Grow Together

Whether you've been friends for years or you just met at a chakra-cleansing class, it's important to get on the same page energetically. For the most part, that just means spending time together, and it doesn't matter what the hell you're doing. But if you really want to change the world, then you've got to spend some of that time getting better at this shit, together. There are plenty of ways that you can grow as friends and as witches. Pick a few that speak to your crew and a few that get you out of your fucking comfort zone.

### ✦ Get Your Ass Moving

Doing movement-based activities together can help you get into your bodies (where the magic is) and out of your heads (where magic goes to die at the hands of doubt and anxiety). You can go full cardio and dance it out or work your arms with some kayaking while you commune with nature. Yoga's a pretty obvious choice, and it's even better if someone in your coven can lead the group. After all, leaning on each other is what it's all about. And why not throw some meditation in there for good measure? It's not movement, but it will definitely help you get out of your head.

### ✧ Learn Something

You now have one of the most amazing resources at your fingertips—a group of incredible people who want to change the world. You'll be amazed at what you can learn from each other. Share your individual knowledge so that it can become collective knowledge and share your experiences so that everyone can come to understand things from a new perspective. By teaching each other, you'll discover what you still want (and need) to learn as a group. Whether you lead the group, take a class, or Google witchy blogs, just make sure you're learning and growing your magical skills *together*.

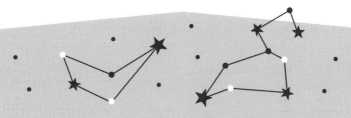

## KNOW YOUR SH*T ABOUT ASTROLOGY

Think astrology's for basic bitches? Think again. Witches are just as ruled by the stars as they are by the moon. Learning about astrology can be a great way to learn more about yourself and each other. And while a basic bitch won't look past her sun sign, you and your sisters can do deep dives into your charts. (No need to pay a professional astrologer—you can find a ton of free tools online.) Then go one step further by keeping an astrology journal and noting how you feel during specific phases of the moon.

# Netflix and Casting

Coming together as a coven doesn't have to be all spiritual growth and skill building. Sharing any kind of experience—even if it's just a movie-night viewing of *The Craft* franchise—is a great way to ease into sharing space and opinions. Do something light that you can all agree on, or take turns choosing activities weekly. Whether you all love the activity or spend the whole time rolling your fucking eyes at it, you're going to learn things about each other that will serve you well when you're working a spell together later. For right now, just let flavorless licorice and stale popcorn work their spells on you.

### ✦ Relax Together

Group-style self-care and downtime is important not just for becoming a cohesive coven but also as a way to gear up for future fights. Save up your energy while you align it by listening to witchy podcasts, brunching it up, or watching a sappy movie (to help you grow emotionally, of course). Have a spa night where you sip signature cocktails made with moon water (page 93). Whatever helps you guys recharge your batteries, make it a habit. Come back to self-care rituals often to re-energize during and after each magical challenge. And, of course, just take some nights off to just be sisters and chill.

### ✦ Work Together, Witches

You have to dip your toes into magical waters before you can head for the damn high dive. Although you might be able to perform a healing ritual with your eyes closed, you could find yourself faltering in a group. The only way to find out if you're good as a team is to (wait for it) work as a team. But keep it light for now. Practice energy work together. Perform tarot readings on each other. Hell, even cooking together can set you up. Food is nourishment for the soul. Plus, all that recipe following and experimenting with ingredients is good practice for spellwork.

### ✧ Normalize Talking to Each Other

It probably goes without saying (ironically), but you should have a dialogue going while doing most of these things. (Not during the meditation, obviously.) Sure, you can learn a lot about a person just by watching them perform any of these suggestions. But understanding someone—what drives them, what scares them, what one-of-a-kind magic they bring to the world—takes *listening* to them. Give each member the space and support to feel comfortable letting the rest of you in. Fostering open and honest conversations right from the jump is going to transform friends into sisters and help you make beautiful magic together.

# WITCH, YOU GOT THIS!

Whether you've been friends for life or you found each other just days ago, it's important to nail the group dynamics before you go playing with literal fucking fire. You need to learn how to navigate the world (and all of its bullshit) as a team.

Tap into nature's magic
Look for shared experiences
Use movement to clear your heads
Get better at shit together
Make time for downtime
Add self-care to your coven's routine
Go easy on the magic (literally)

You don't need to do trust falls or anything. But getting to know what makes your sisters tick can help your energies harmonize for far more effective spellwork in the long run.

# PART TWO

# BECOME A KICKASS COVEN

"Women should
be in charge
of everything."

—— ⟨ • ⟩ ——

LILITH, *CHAOS*

# CHAPTER 7

# GET YOUR SH*T TOGETHER

**Y**ou've got the who and why figured out. Now you just need to figure out the what, where, when, and how. You're thinking, "Oh, *is that all*?!" Relax. You've already done the hard work. This is just your basic setup. So, break out the binder tabs! Kidding. This really isn't going to be that much work. If you're not a planner, someone else in your group sure as hell is. Let them organize things (as long as they're cool with it) while you work on the big-picture stuff. Being able to play to each person's strengths will be your coven's secret weapon when you're working to change the world.

## The Technical Sh*t

Groups do better with a little structure, especially where magic is involved. Just look at nature. It may look like beautiful chaos, but nothing in nature is random. And having a plan from the start means you don't have to think about any of this shit later. It also gives you something to point to when a member goes rogue and wants to hold your weekly meeting at Al's Pancakes when you specifically said you were a diehard Waffles 'N' Things girl. But really, there's no need to be all, "that's not what the book says" about your coven's structure. Decide on some basics now and be flexible later.

### ✦ What's Your Practice Look Like?

You've been working on your vision for your coven from Day One, so you should have a pretty good idea of what it's all about. But have you considered which traditions you'd like to observe? It's OK if the answer is No. Mull them over now and keep them in mind as you read on.

- **What kind of witchcraft will you practice?**
- **Will you pray to a particular god or goddess?**
- **Will you observe Wiccan holidays?**

Witchcraft's inclusivity is one of its greatest strengths, so you can absolutely march to the beat of your own drummer. But if you feel pulled to follow the tenets of a particular religion, then now's a good time to explore that.

### ✦ Want a Hierarchy?

It's not uncommon for covens to use a hierarchy that positions people based on their experience with both magic and the coven itself. Some have degrees (like Dedicant, Neophyte, and Initiant) that dictate how involved people are in the rituals and how much say they have in the coven's work. If that feels a little too "corporate America" to you, you're not alone. Plenty of covens come in a more democratic flavor. But you get to do whatever the hell works for you. If you want to sort yourselves in Hogwarts houses, go for it. A big coven might need some structure. Four witches hanging out? Not so much.

## Words to Live By

By this point, you know that even the simplest words can wield a fuck-ton of magic. And there are a lot of them in the craft. Sure, there are intentions and spells. But there are also bylaws and grimoires. Not to mention the words we use to describe ourselves. So let's start here: Are you a witch, or not? If the word "witch" feels off for any reason, use one that feels comfortable or powerful to you. Once you've sorted that out, move on to the written shit. And remember,

## PRACTICAL MAGIC

Some covens have a strict schedule for their rituals, usually based on the lunar calendar. If that's your thing, have at it. But if you like to keep it low-key, that's okay, too. It's your fucking coven. Your weekly ritual can be Magic and Milkshakes. Or maybe you ramp up your magical activities around important political races instead of Wiccan holidays. You get to decide. But you're a group of grown-ass adults with real adult obligations, so flexibility is probably a fucking virtue here. Make sure your schedule meets everyone's needs.

there's no magical law that says you can't collaborate on a Google doc. Make it work for you.

### ✧ Bylaws

Those questions you read a little bit earlier? You don't need to know the answers yet, but you will when you go to write up your bylaws. These are the guidelines your coven will abide by. They can be as basic or flexible as you need them to be, so start with what you know and fill in the rest later. Some things to include are:

- A mission statement
- Membership requirements
- Your hierarchy (if any)
- Your meeting schedule
- Traditions followed
- Guiding principles
- Exit strategies for members
- A member agreement

If you don't go the digital route, make sure everyone in the coven has access to your bylaws. Some covens make members sign the agreement. That might be a bit much, but at least have them acknowledge they've read the damn thing.

### ✦ Book of Shadows

A Book of Shadows (a.k.a. BOS, grimoire, magical diary, or mirror book) is like a badass scrapbook of your magical journey. It'll usually include your bylaws, rituals, spells, events, and general information pertaining to your crew, but it's really up to you. There's no end-all-be-all BOS. Each coven creates their own, and you can get *really* creative with it. Turn it into organized chaos, bullet-journal style. Have the most artistic witch among you add awesome illustrations. You can even buy really cool, old-timey pages of spells and rituals online. Of course, you can also just keep it easy and go completely digital. (Then no one has to remember where the fucking book ended up.)

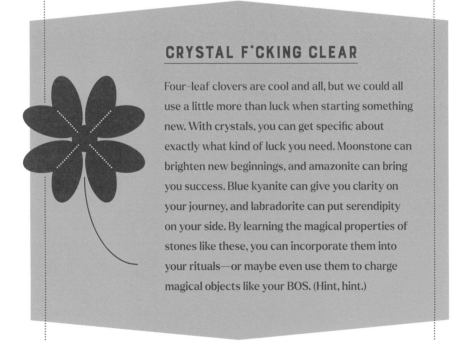

## CRYSTAL F*CKING CLEAR

Four-leaf clovers are cool and all, but we could all use a little more than luck when starting something new. With crystals, you can get specific about exactly what kind of luck you need. Moonstone can brighten new beginnings, and amazonite can bring you success. Blue kyanite can give you clarity on your journey, and labradorite can put serendipity on your side. By learning the magical properties of stones like these, you can incorporate them into your rituals—or maybe even use them to charge magical objects like your BOS. (Hint, hint.)

# Make a Damn Plan

People have fucking lives outside of the coven. You can't just say, "We'll get together sometime next week" and assume it'll work out. (Looking at you, Pisceans.) Schedule your shit with everyone's input or you can't get pissed off when someone doesn't show. Start by designating one day a week (or month) to meet up. You can always get together as needed, but scheduling a regular meeting that people can put in their calendars makes it more likely everyone will attend. Whether you want to meet on Tuesday nights for wine and witchcraft or on every full moon for a crystal ritual, that's your business.

### ✦ Get a Big-Ass Planner

Find the witch among you whose happy place is the office-supply section of any given store and put them in charge of the calendar. (No shame if it's you.) Let them choose a big-ass planner—the kind with stickers and a fun cover. Bonus points if it already includes little icons for the phases of the moon, because you're going to have to write those in there anyway. You're also going to need space for both the magical shit and the everyday shit, from Wiccan holidays to senate races. You'll use this planner to work out all the things you want to do. You can always add them to your digital calendars once they're finalized, but you need a fucking point of reference so you don't lose your minds in today's too-busy world.

### ✦ Sketch Out Some Agendas

You should have at least a rough agenda for each meeting so you don't end up eating wings and watching football the whole night when you're supposed to be taking advantage of the full moon. Use the planner (or a few pieces of scrap paper and the calendar on your phone) to sketch out what you want at least the next few meetings to look like. Include any lessons taught by members, plans for future activism, and rituals you want to perform. And don't forget the really important shit, like deciding who's responsible for bringing the wine.

# Carve Out a Sacred Space

Have you ever heard of a covenstead? That's the technical term for wherever the hell it is your coven calls home. If that's the all-night diner with the really good disco fries, so be it. But, ideally, you'll want to have one space that acts as base camp for your coven even if you spend most of your time at the diner anyway. Some covens go so far as to rent a space, but many either pick one person's home or rotate between a few. Then you just have to decide on the dress code. No, seriously. A traditional coven might require members to wear robes or go "skyclad" (yep: naked). Don't worry—you can stick to yoga pants.

### ✧ To Host

Deciding whether you'll host or the meeting places will rotate may depend more on your general tolerance for people and less on any magical *accoutrement* your home can offer. That's totally reasonable. You would need to be cool with cleaning up after people, fronting any money, people being in your space, organizing activities (including flammable ones), and communicating with everyone. It's a lot. But if you were born for that kind of shit, or your house really does offer some sort of magical accoutrement, go for it. Just get the money stuff sorted so you're not resentful later.

### ✧ Or Not to Host

Picking a place that isn't your house can be both a relief and an anxiety-inducing nightmare of logistics—especially for control freaks. (Shoutout to the Virgos!) If you don't want the burden, make sure you set up your coven to share it. This is about cooperative magic, after all. Play to everyone's strengths and be mindful of their weaknesses. If a member's house looks like it belongs to hoarders, that shit's going to block the flow of energy. Pick someone who's into feng shui to host. And remember, you can always go to the diner. It's clean and there's coffee.

### ✧ Cleanse the Space

Once you decide on a meeting space, you'll need to cleanse it and prepare it for new, collaborative energy. Use the cleansing ritual at the end of this chapter with the intention to start fresh and have successful, productive meetings. Not a fan of burning herbs? Try diffusing an essential oil instead. And if you simply hate the *smell* of herbs, spritz some rosewater around the place instead. Just remember to charge the space with positivity when you're done. (And never burn herbs around pets or small children with respiratory issues.)

## KNOW YOUR SH*T ABOUT SMUDGING

A lot of people believe that smudging is a witchy tradition, but this particular ritual of smoke cleansing is actually exclusive to Native American cultures. The cultural appropriation of smudging is harmful to Native communities, to whom the practice is sacred. Smudge sticks, which have come to represent the pain and compulsory sacrifice of Native peoples, are being sold at every trendy store these days alongside another sacred herb: Palo Santo. Their commercialization ignores the ritual's true and traumatic history, and the money never makes it back to the Native peoples whose spiritual traditions were ripped from them. So skip the white sage bundles and look for a cleansing ritual that taps into your own heritage instead.

## Make Magic Anywhere

Wherever you meet should fuel your coven's vibe. That could be your favorite brunch place, or a relaxing spot on the beach. That might even be the middle of the fucking woods, if you want to be closer to nature and are bizarrely unafraid of spiders. Just know your local ordinances and closing times, and always obey

"No Trespassing" signs. If you're going to practice some graveside magic à la *Now and Then*, remember to blow out any candles and pick up after yourselves. Oh yeah, and don't piss off the fucking dead. Respectful light magic only.

## Make Magic Separately

We learned during the 2020 pandemic that video-conferencing software is fucking magic. So have members call in from their personal altar or ask them to at least have a few magical items nearby. They can use crystals, candles, and incense to feel like they're part of the circle. Open the meeting with a mantra said or read aloud as one to help you connect and get you into the right energy space, and close things out the same way. Otherwise, run the meeting as usual.

## Create a Kickass Ritual Altar

Witches put a lot of pressure on themselves to have Instagram-worthy altars. But all you really need is a little nook with a few objects that make you feel connected to magic and your purpose. Although you'll each have your own personal altars at home (or at least you should), you'll want to have a ritual altar at your covenstead. This should include all the shit you need to make magic together, like your:

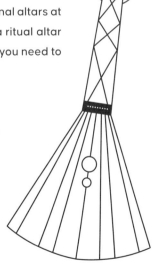

- **Book of Shadows**
- **Altar bowl/cauldron/fire-safe bowl/Dutch oven**
- **Besom**
- **Wand or athame (a sort of ceremonial knife)**
- **Candles and incense**
- **Various crystals**
- **Divination tools**
- **Herbs**
- **Personal tokens**

Members can also bring stuff from home, especially if they want it charged by the energy of the coven. That can include personal tokens, crystals, or divination tools as well as spell jars and talismans. Because you're focused on magical activism, you'll probably want to include a few items that remind you of your activist goals. (Anything from an "I Voted" sticker to a pink hat will do.) You'll learn more about what the hell this stuff does in the next section. But keep in mind that these items are just enhancements. The magic comes from you!

## WITCH, YOU GOT THIS!

You know what you want. Now you just have to put it all together in some sort of cohesive way that everyone can understand. This is where the rubber meets the road: you're creating a framework for your coven that will help you to get shit done so you can change the fucking world. So, as annoying as paperwork can be, just fucking do it.

Decide what your coven's about
Choose how you'll practice
Write it all down
Make a fucking plan for your time
Choose your meeting spot(s)
Meet on the go when you need to
Create a kickass shared altar

Even a basic framework is better than no framework. You can always add color later (literally, if you like that sort of thing), when you're a little deeper into your journey.

# A GOOD, OLD-FASHIONED
## ◇◇ CLEANSING ◇◇

Hey, if it ain't broke, don't fix it. There's a lot to be said for bringing magic into the 21st century, but some things are better left un-fucked-with. You want to clear a space of negative energy, you burn some cleansing herbs. The smoke not only clears out the crap, it also helps you bless the space and everyone in it with the properties of the plants you choose.

If you've always been curious about how to cleanse a space like a proper, old-school witch, here's your chance to find out. As with all things magical, it's more about your intention than it is about any properties the physical objects might possess. Keep that in mind from the moment you grab your materials.

### MAGICAL MATERIALS

Bundle of cleansing herbs like:

   Sage

   Rosemary

   Cedar

   Juniper

   Lavender

   Thyme

White candle

Matches or lighter

Fire-safe bowl

Bowl of sand

### CLEVER WITCH TIP
Cultures around the world have burned herbs or incense in cleansing rituals. Do a little digging into your ancestry and see which herbs speak to your heritage.

## 1: Slow Things Down

Before you even reach for your materials, connect with that cleansing energy. Move slowly and purposefully toward your goal of ousting all the energy-draining shit in the space.

## 2: Have an Intention at the Ready

When you clear out the crap, you leave a sort of energetic vacuum. What do you want to fill it with? Have an intention ready to go so that your newly cleansed space feels the way you want it to.

## 3: Open Things Up

The negative energy has to have some-where to go. If you don't want it going into your cat, open up as many windows and doors as you can. (This can also help with the smell. Burning herbs can be strong AF.)

## 4: Cleanse the Place

Stand at the doorway (your front door or the doorway to the space) and light the candle, then use the candle to light the bundle of herbs. You're going to keep your intention in your mind and the bundle in your hand while you slowly move clockwise around the edge of the entire space or house, making sure the smoke gets into every crack and crevice—yes, including that over-stuffed closet. Hold the bowl under the herbs while you walk so you don't get ash on the fucking carpet.

## 5: Do It Together

When working this ritual with a coven, have everyone use sound to help you clear out stubborn energy blocks. As you walk around, you'll notice the sound is dull in certain places—those are your blocks. Just clap your hands or jingle your keys at them. Hell, you can have Siri play some Lizzo if that's the vibe you want for the space.

## 6: Close the Ceremony

When you arrive back at the front door or entryway, close your eyes and see the space filled with bright white light. Repeat your intention one last time, extinguish the herbs in the bowl of sand, and then go about your life.

### MAGICAL MOD

Holding a burning bundle of herbs and filling your home with smoke is not for everyone. That's totally fine, because there are about a dozen other ways to cleanse a space. You can place a selenite crystal by doorways or spritz rooms with rosewater (blessed by you). And *Hocus Pocus* had it right—if you need to dispel negative energy in a hurry, just use regular old table salt. But maybe put it in a bowl instead of throwing it on the floor like a sleep-deprived teenager.

"The world is full of magic things, patiently waiting for our senses to grow sharper."

W.B. YEATS

# CHAPTER 8

# AMP UP YOUR MAGIC

**E**very action has power if you intend it to. You can set an intention to have a great day when you wake up in the morning. You can set an intention to get rid of the toxic crap in your life when you take out the actual trash. You can set an intention while putting on the watermelon lip balm you keep in your car so that your words carry its sweetness. You don't *need* another damn thing to set that intention. But if you want to amplify your power, magical objects, spells, rituals, and methods can help. They can also put you in the right headspace to get shit done. After all, what we believe works, works.

## Symbols and Sh*t

Symbols, talismans, and their slightly more intentional cousin, sigils, are some of the simplest things you can use to focus or amplify your magic. With talismans, you ascribe meaning to an object. With symbols and sigils, it's literally just you, a magic marker, and a piece of paper here. In fact, you don't even have to draw the symbol yourself for you to imbue it with your intention. It could be on a fucking bumper sticker for all it matters. Know why? Well, remember Gary Hallet's badass ghost-hand-burning badge in *Practical Magic*? Symbols and talismans have power because we believe they have power. That's the important part—our belief. If you want to believe a soda can is good luck, then it will be. How easy is that?

## ✦ Symbols

A symbol is just a thing (usually drawn) that stands for something else. And symbols are incredibly important in activism, magical or not. The fist on BLM posters stands for solidarity with oppressed peoples. The rainbow flag represents the diversity of, and support for, the LGBTQ+ community. The peace sign, well, pretty much speaks for itself. One glance at any of these symbols, and you understand the importance of what they represent and feel the emotion behind them.

You can use those symbols in your spellwork, or you can create your own. As long as it has meaning to you, it will carry your intention. Draw it on your important papers, use it as your profile pic, add it to a talisman, draw it on your body, wear it in face paint, get it inked over your heart—whichever method is most meaningful to you is the one that will work the best for you.

## ✦ Sigils

Sigils are symbols crafted from the components of a written intention. Basically, you think about what you want, turn that into a short phrase you can write down, then remove the vowels and repeating consonants. What you're left with is a bunch of arcs and lines, which you then incorporate into a sort of DIY symbol. Connect the lines however the hell you want to, taking some creative liberties wherever you need to in order to get a symbol you're happy with.

The goal here isn't a pretty picture. That's what symbols are for. In fact, sigils are a little awkward-looking and messy as often as they are neat. But it doesn't fucking matter because you've infused every line with your intention. Put it somewhere you'll see it and get used to it so it fades into the background. Or paint over it. Or bury it. Whatever. Just move on with your life and let it become a part of you that you don't even think about.

### ✦ Talismans

Think of a talisman as the physical version of a symbol. It's an object, often ordinary and non-magical, that you have imbued with power (either physically, by charging it, or emotionally, by believing it). That worry stone your mom keeps in her purse? Talisman. That rabbit's foot on your uncle's keychain? Gross fucking talisman. That rose-quartz crystal on your bathroom sink? Talisman! (In fact, crystals are some of the most common talismans around.) And yes, as Sally says, even Detective Hallet's standard-issue badge is a talisman. You can charge a talisman through spellwork and rituals, but it's really not necessary. Simply looking at the thing and deciding it's a talisman makes it one. That's just how intention works. (But it can't hurt to add a little extra magic to the mix.)

## PRACTICAL MAGIC

Whenever you get a new magical item, whether it's a crystal or a cauldron, you want to cleanse it. You don't know where shit has been before you bought it, or whose dirty negative energy is all over it. Everything should get a fresh start when it gets to you. There are a lot of ways to cleanse objects and spaces, so just pick the one that works for you. You can use the smoke of cleansing scents (like cedar or rosemary), water (for water-safe objects), salt, sunlight, moonlight, or sound. Whichever method you use, just hold your intention to give your object a clean slate while you use it.

# Magical Amplifiers

As you work your way through *The Kickass Coven*, you'll notice there are a fuck-ton of ways to give your intention a magical boost. Some tap into the energy of nature or spirits, while others use the magical properties of objects. Choose the methods that speak to you for your specific purpose. Starting a new venture? Do it under the new moon. Off to a protest? Take a piece of protective black tourmaline with you. Using any of these magical amplifiers will imbue your intention with a little something extra. And if you just want to indulge in some magical retail therapy, go for it. Candles, crystals, and essential oils can be just as fun as they are powerful.

### ✧ The Moon

No matter which traditions a witch follows, they likely revere the moon. Its powerful, tide-moving energy can amplify your inner magic every day of the year, but it can be incredibly helpful to tailor your spellwork to specific lunar phases. Each one brings its own unique energy to the mix. (But more on that later.) In fact, the moon might be affecting your magic even when you don't realize it. If you ever have a spell fall a little flat, consider first whether the moon's particular phase that night might have had an impact. (Then also consider whether you worked your spell while hangry. That'll get you every damn time.)

### ✧ Prayer

One of the benefits of that all-inclusive ideology of witchcraft is that you can reach out to any spirit, ancestor, god, or goddess you feel connected to (or want to feel connected to). Many witches pray to the Triple Goddess, a primary deity in Wiccan faith. But if you want to call upon the spirit of actress and brilliant inventor Hedy Lamarr for inspiration when faced with a complex problem, you can do that. If you want to ask Hermes, Greek messenger god, for help communicating, go for it. There's also no rule in witchcraft that says you can't follow the tenets of a major religion and pray to its deities while working spells. Do what feels right to you.

## ✦ Mantras

Mantras are words or sounds meant to be repeated (aloud or in your head) to help you concentrate on a specific goal or thought—and sometimes, like in meditation, to help you not concentrate on anything. If magic is all about setting an intention, then mantras are all about holding onto that intention and willing it into existence. Put another way, mantras are mini spells. You can add their repetition to a ritual to focus or amplify your intention, or you can repeat them daily to manifest something big. You can also use them in their more self-helpy (but still totally badass) form, as affirmations that you say to yourself to bring about personal change.

## ✦ Candles

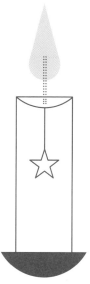

Candles and magic go together like peanut butter and bananas. (Hey, don't knock it 'til you try it.) But did you know that they do more than just set the mood? First and foremost, they bring light to your desires. But they can also help you manifest different desires based on their color. And by anointing them with oils and herbs, you can turn candles into even more powerful intention transmitters. When a spell calls for a simple white candle (as many do, because it's the most versatile), that doesn't necessarily mean a *boring* white candle. As long as the wax is white, the container can say whatever the hell you want it to. There are plenty of inspiringly sweary ones out there.

Whichever kind you buy, just don't burn the place down with them. Lots of rituals ask that you let your candle burn out completely. For those, you should buy ones made for the job (literally "spell candles," which are small and thin with a short burn time) and stay with them while they burn. When you do put candles out, use a snuffer. Never blow them out or you might blow away your intention. And—it should go without fucking saying—never burn a candle near flammable shit.

### ✧ Crystal Work

A good crystal focuses your mind and amplifies your intention. That's why you'll see them strewn all over the damn book. If you're not into them or don't have them, don't worry about it. They're not for everyone, and they're not going to make or break your spellwork. But they can be a fun, easy way to give your rituals a boost, support your magical activism, and add a bit of magic to your everyday adventures in adulting.

Each stone offers a number of helpful properties, so definitely do a deeper dive on this handy little magical amplifier later. Then get creative with how you incorporate them into your spellwork, from creating gorgeous crystal grids to infusing your morning cup of java with something more powerful than stevia. Just make sure you cleanse your crystals regularly. Not all of them are water-safe, but you can pop them in the window to soak up some cleansing sunlight.

### ✧ Essential Oils

Essential oils are concentrated plant extracts (with the same magical properties as the plants themselves) that are distilled into cute little amber bottles. Unless you live under a very boring-smelling rock, you've probably come across them a time or two. It's pretty common these days to find them in store-bought candles and cleaning products as well as sold individually for personal use. Diffusing is one way to use these oils in your spellwork. You can also use them to anoint candles or tools for your rituals or to anoint yourself before taking action. And of course, you can use them to make a mean bar of soap or scent a warm bath for some magical "me time."

The dark bottle is important because it keeps sunlight from penetrating the glass and spoiling the oil. (Some oils—usually citrusy ones—are also photosensitive, meaning they can cause a reaction on your skin if exposed to sunlight. So take care.) For anything outside of diffusing, you'll want to dilute your oils in a carrier oil. This could be whatever oil you normally cook with or something a little more refined like jojoba oil. As long as you know what the hell you're doing, essential oils are a safe and lovely smelling way to give your magic a boost. But—and this part's important—if you ever spill a pure oil like peppermint on your skin, quickly rub olive oil into it to avoid a reaction. Water will do absolutely fucking nothing.

## ✧ Potions and Tinctures

Potions and tinctures are magical concoctions made by using herbs, crystals, and usually a good amount of alcohol. They generally go down your throat or on your skin. And for that reason, we don't fuck with them in this book. This is a subject that, if it interests you, is worth digging into properly—safety precautions and all. Potions and tinctures can be positive, healing, and utterly delightful magical creations that help with a range of issues. But suffice it to say: just as we do not hex people, we do not poison them or give them a gross-looking rash, either intentionally or unintentionally, because we fucked with something we had no business fucking with based on a brief Wikipedia description.

## ✧ Herbs, Spices, and Other Plants

Just like crystals, plants can imbue your spellwork with their magical properties. Unlike crystals, they can also make a room smell utterly divine (sometimes literally—gods and goddesses have been known to show a fondness for particular scents). From burning bundles and incense to anointing candles with essential oils and ground herbs, you'll see plants used in any number of ways throughout your magical adventures. And each one has multiple magical properties that can benefit your intention. When a ritual calls for an herb you don't have on hand, see what you can get your hands on locally. Then look up their meanings to see if any align with the intention of the spell. Just don't ingest any plants without talking to a healthcare provider.

## KNOW YOUR SH'T ABOUT ANIMALS

Rule #1: Don't burn shit or use essential oils around pets, who have more sensitive respiratory systems than we do. Rule #2: Leave animals out of your spellwork. The whole "eye of newt" thing is part of a pretty pervasive myth about witchcraft going hand-in-hand with devil worship. Really, witches have a deep and loving respect for all living things and would never harm an animal. So if you go to the grocery store and buy a cow's tongue for some weird spell you found online, you've gone too fucking far. (And let's not even get into Michelle Pfeiffer in *Stardust.*)

## Divination Tools

If you've read *Harry Potter and the Prisoner of Azkaban*, you're basically an expert in divination already. (Maybe even more of one than Professor Trelawney.) But assuming you haven't. . . . Divination is the art of uncovering the unknown by magical means. Look it up online and you'll find at least a couple hundred methods of divination—way too fucking many to worry about. Trust that you'll come across particular ones at the right time. For now, we'll start with a few of the basics. Just remember that the tool is only ever part of the equation. It's really just a transmitter, so you'll need to work on honing your intuition before trying out any crystal balls.

### ✦ Tarot Cards

Like astrology, tarot cards get a bad rap for being basic, or even some kind of parlor trick. But they can be a really useful magical tool if you know how to use them. You can't just read descriptions out of the little booklet that comes with them and call it a day. Sure, that's a good way to start out. But then you need to learn to tap into your intuition and read between the lines.

Although tarot cards can be a serious divination tool, you are allowed to have a little fun. For one thing, don't just buy the standard pack—there are a ton of styles to choose from. And for another, do some lighthearted readings, especially until you get the hang of things. Even when you're not actually divining things, the cards can still help you make connections you might have otherwise missed.

### ✦ Tea Leaves

The reading of tea leaves (a.k.a. tasseography) is, well, that—the art of reading into the shapes made by your tea leaves when you're about finished with a cup of tea. As with all divination, you'll want to quiet your mind, get centered, and tap into your intuition before focusing on the leaves. You can choose to see what message the Universe has for you, or you can ask a direct question and interpret the leaves for an answer.

Put a spoonful of loose-leaf tea in your cup, pour hot water over it, and drink it almost all the way up. (You need a little liquid to move the leaves. And no, cutting open a bag of Lipton won't work for this.) Start to form your intention while the tea steeps, then continue to mull it over in your mind as you sip. When you're finished drinking, you'll swirl the cup several times before inverting it onto the saucer and reading the leaves. This is one of those rituals that seems easy but is actually pretty involved, so you'll want to look for in-depth directions or ask your friendly neighborhood astrologer for some help.

### ✦ Runes and Ogham

Runes and Ogham are actually the letters of two different old-timey alphabets. In divination, you'll often find the runic alphabet on tiles or stones and the Ogham alphabet on wooden staves made from a variety of sacred trees. Although they come from two different cultures, they're pretty damn similar in look and purpose. You interpret a spread of runes or staves just like you'd interpret a spread of tarot cards. So basically, runes and Ogham are to tarot what Rummikub is to gin rummy. Because the spiritual meanings of Ogham

are closely related to that of sacred trees, this divination tool is a good one for nature-loving witches.

## ✧ Pendulums

You may have already tried this one out in the earlier chapters, where it's included because it can be as fun as it is simple. A pendulum is a divination tool with a small, slightly heavy object hanging from a string or cord. It can be made of pretty much any material, but a lot of them use a crystal or piece of metal at the bottom. (In fact, you can find some really gorgeous handcrafted ones online.) This tool relies on your intuitive energy traveling down the cord to swing the pendulum in circles when it has something to say.

When you first get your pendulum, cleanse it, charge it with your intention to find clarity, and then let it channel your energy to give you the answers you seek. The great thing about this divination tool is that you can use it both for answering those all-important questions *and* for finding shit, whether you're in need of something or you've just misplaced it. Its beauty lies in its simplicity—it can only answer "yes" or "no." Ask it a question, get a direct answer. Move it over a map (even one that looks like it was drawn in crayon by a toddler), and see where you get a "yes," like you're playing a magical game of Hot and Cold. It's the perfect tool for the beginner-witch's altar.

## ✧ Scrying

Scrying is less a tool than a method, but it gets a pass because it's the method everyone thinks of when they think of divination. Yep, you guessed it—those fortune tellers waving their hands dramatically over a crystal ball are scrying. But you don't actually need the crystal ball. A mirror, a flame, a bowl of water, or any other reflective surface will do. Again, your intuition and energy are key here.

Scrying is a lot like staring at fluffy, white clouds on a blue-sky day and finding discernable shapes. Everyone's interpretation is going to be different.

What you're really doing is giving your intuition a canvas to paint. You see what you're meant to see. The trick is not to try too hard. Clear your mind, focus on your intention, and relax your eyes. You might see full images, or you might just see shapes and shadows. Keep a pen and paper handy and write down whatever pops into your head. Afterward, see if you notice any themes. And don't fucking force it—you'll scare off your intuition.

## WITCH, YOU GOT THIS!

Do you need candles and crystals and cauldrons (oh my!) to practice magic? Of course not. You are magic. Can they help you focus and amplify that magic? Yes. Are they fun to use? Also yes. So why not try out a few of the ones that speak to you?

Use symbols and sigils for a quick, easy boost
Follow the phases of the moon
Bring light to your intentions with candles
Manifest specific desires using crystals and herbs
See the future in tarot cards and tea leaves
Swing for the stars with a pretty pendulum
Treat animals with fucking respect

This is just a quick overview of a few of the tools available to badass magical activists like yourself. Just imagine what you can do when you master the damn things!

"A little magic
can take you
a long way."

— ⟨•⟩ —

ROALD DAHL

# CHAPTER 9

# MARK YOUR WITCHY CALENDAR

**Y**ou are magic (just in case that hasn't sunk in yet). But that doesn't mean you have to rely solely on your own power to get shit done. Learning how to harness the energy of the world around you—the energy of the entire fucking Universe, in fact—gives you an endless supply of the stuff. And one of the easiest ways to do that is to keep an eye on the calendar. That's possibly even easier than using crystals. From the phases of the moon to traditional witchy holidays, the heightened energy of these natural cycles can fuel your everyday magic and your activist goals. Add to that the energy of the dates and traditions that are special to you and your coven in particular, and you've got a hell of a lot of magical backup.

## The Wheel of the Year

The Wheel of the Year is a symbol used throughout witchy traditions to represent the eight pagan holidays as eight equal pieces of an ever-turning wheel. The holidays themselves mark the start of natural cycles that the pagans were thrilled to realize returned every year. With each, some things are lost and others are gained, but the wheel keeps turning. The pagans found that comforting. So take a page out of their book and let it help you feel just as grounded in the world (and in your magic).

You can adapt the wheel to however it works best for you—remove anything you're not feeling, add any other traditions you like. Each of these cycles comes with its own particular energy, so even if you choose not to celebrate them, understanding them can help you make the most of their magic. Just keep in mind that these dates are for the northern hemisphere. Much like sink water, they run opposite down south.

## ✦ Samhain

Samhain may mean "summer's end," but this holiday kicks off the witchy year on October 31st. (Come on. Of course our year starts on Halloween!) On that day, the veil between the dead and the living is at its thinnest, so it's a good day to communicate with and honor the dead. Offerings are pretty common on Samhain, so pour one out for the Triple Goddess and your great aunt Ida.

For six months afterward, the dead have a stronger sway over the Earth. Of course, that's not as stark as it seems. It's just the start of the colder months, when the nights are longest and the plants die back, giving the appearance of a world gone to sleep. It's a period of rest, so work some fucking "me time" into that hectic schedule of yours.

## ✦ Yule

Before there was Christmas, with all its pageantry, there was Yule, the simple celebration of the Winter Solstice. Yule runs from December 20th to the 25th. And if you feel all warm and fuzzy at the thought of snow and holiday lights like Kevin McAllister, you still get to decorate a tree. In fact, that tradition dates back to Yule and was used to celebrate the infinite nature of deities (hence the evergreen).

Yule symbolizes rebirth and renewal, so it's a great time to set some intentions for personal growth, like expanding your coven's outreach. And it's a great time for any spellwork relating to rejuvenation. Because the holiday includes the shortest, darkest day of the year, it's also known to be a good time for divination and communing with the dead.

### ✦ Imbolc

February 1st and 2nd bring you Imbolc (literally, "in the belly"), the celebration of the pregnancy-like period between Winter Solstice and Spring Equinox. With spring right around the corner, Imbolc represents a time of fertility and carries a message of optimism for the future. Use this holiday's hopeful energy to work spells for positive change and fresh starts. (If you can swing it, it would be a good time to start your coven!)

Imbolc is a fire festival, but there's no need to torch the place. If you really want to celebrate, light a candle while you spring-clean your house. And then finish celebrating with a relaxing, candle-lit bath to give yourself a clean slate, too. You're a badass magical activist. You deserve it!

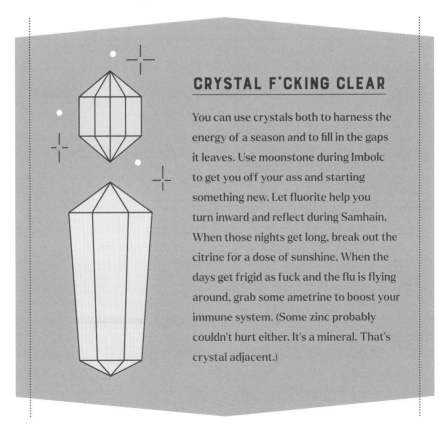

## CRYSTAL F'CKING CLEAR

You can use crystals both to harness the energy of a season and to fill in the gaps it leaves. Use moonstone during Imbolc to get you off your ass and starting something new. Let fluorite help you turn inward and reflect during Samhain. When those nights get long, break out the citrine for a dose of sunshine. When the days get frigid as fuck and the flu is flying around, grab some ametrine to boost your immune system. (Some zinc probably couldn't hurt either. It's a mineral. That's crystal adjacent.)

## ✧ Ostara

Have you ever wondered why Easter—a Christian holiday that has nothing to do with rabbits and eggs—is celebrated with, you know, rabbits and eggs? That's because the holiday was basically superimposed on the pagan tradition of Ostara. Also known as the Spring Equinox, Ostara runs from March 20th to the 23rd and is celebrated as a time of fertility (rabbits) and rebirth (eggs).

This is also a fertile time for magic, especially when it comes to new endeavors. Spellwork that involves the growth, blossoming, and amplification of things can definitely benefit from Ostara's energy. Spend some time around this holiday making plans for your magical activism, too, and ask the goddess Ostara to bless them (with an appropriate offering, of course).

## ✧ Beltane

Imbolc and Ostara may offer hope of great things to come, but Beltane (celebrated from April 30th to May 1st) is the official start of summer and six months of the living having stronger sway than the dead. That's pretty damn hopeful, too. This one's about celebrating life and magic. It's also about shedding those pesky inhibitions and indulging a little. Let loose and enjoy! When Beltane comes around, things are starting to get lighter, brighter, and easier. Use this time to work spells that rely on sunlight as well as spells that bring joy. Keep in mind, too, that magical plants are also blossoming, so make sure you take advantage of them at their peak.

## ✧ Litha

Litha (a.k.a. Summer Solstice) runs from June 20th to the 22nd and includes the longest day of the year. It celebrates the triumph of light over darkness—right before the world starts to descend into darkness again. Those pagans were really "glass half full" people, and they went all out for this one. Celebrating involves fresh fruit, sweet honey, and feasting. Who can't get behind that?

We're going to call this one the "YOLO" holiday. During Litha, the days begin to grow shorter. So you know you only have a brief time to make the most of that bright-light summer energy. That's why Litha is a big time for magic, with a joyful, shoot-for-the-moon, anything-can-happen kind of vibe that can give your spell-work a kickass boost. But that wheel keeps turning, so take a minute to put your magical tools somewhere they can get a good deep clean from a full day of sunlight before the world goes back to sleep.

### ✧ Lughnasadh

Lughnasadh, which falls on August 1, is your basic late-summer harvest festival. It's a time to reap what you've sown, learn some lessons, and offer your favorite goddess a Honeycrisp (or other fresh fruit). Celebrate by spending some time outside enjoying the waning sunlight and eating freshly baked bread. Or by heading over to your local farmer's market and having a slice of prize-winning pie. Whatever works for you.

Some consider Lughnasadh to be a kind of witchy Thanksgiving, where you think about all you're thankful for and celebrate abundance by eating a shit-ton of delicious food. As a celebration of abundance, it's a good time to work spells asking for just that. Reach out to gods and goddesses of the harvest (like Lugh, the Celtic god for whom the holiday is named) with a small offering for some magical backup. And don't forget to look back on all you've learned and accomplished over the past year!

### ✧ Mabon

The triumph of light that's celebrated during Litha is clearly short lived, because Mabon (a.k.a. the Autumn Equinox) is about darkness returning. But, ever the optimists, pagans celebrate it because they know that life will blossom again in spring. In that spirit, they would offer anointed cornucopias of candles, gourds, and pinecones to the gods and goddesses of light and dark. They also offered tea and food, which was then "returned to the earth" (buried in the ground) to celebrate the cyclical nature of the seasons.

Mabon is the time to reflect on your lessons and how they'll move you forward in the months ahead. Plant the seeds now for the things you hope to manifest in more abundant months to come so that this holiday's energy can imbue them with life. And break out the pumpkin spice. It's a celebration, damn it.

# The Magic of the Moon

Using the phases of the moon to give your magic a boost is like a life hack—one of those "work smarter, not harder" things. Why wouldn't you let the tide-moving magic of an ancient celestial body do some of the heavy lifting for you? Each lunar phase has its own particular magical influence over a range of things. Starting something new? Use that new-moon energy. Performing a healing ritual? Do it under a full moon for an infusion of good health.

Don't worry if the moon isn't where you need it to be when you want to work a spell. Aligning your intention with lunar phases can definitely help, but not doing it won't hurt. And when your gut tells you the timing is right, you gotta listen. Your intuition and your intention are always what matter most to your magic.

### ✧ The New Moon

New-moon energy is like new-car smell: fresh, exciting, and a little bit mysterious. During this first lunar phase, the moon and the sun are perfectly aligned so that the moon is backlit and looks completely black to us here on Earth. As the first of the moon's phases, it's all about new beginnings. Let your imagination go fucking wild. Make big plans; set scary, important goals; and get ready to manifest the shit out of them.

As far as your everyday magic goes, cleansing and creation rituals are especially powerful during this phase. It's also a good time to shake the Etch-A-Sketch and give yourself a clean slate, which means forgiving yourself and others. (And maybe having a relaxing salt-infused soak and letting your troubles drain away.) Your magic will be better for it and you'll be starting the lunar month off in a good place to work some of your most effective magic ever.

### ✧ The Waxing Moon

A waxing moon is a growing moon—the thing is getting bigger and brighter every night. So this is the perfect time to tackle any projects or spellwork around things that you want to expand, like your bank account. It can also help you manifest the really great, intangible stuff like luck, courage, creativity, and love.

The waxing moon can also be ideal for working on yourself, from building up your confidence to shoring up your health. It can give you strength and encourage healing if you set your intentions accordingly. This is a positive, hopeful moon, so give it your dreams. All it asks in return is that you meet it halfway with your actions. Not bad, considering that, as magical activists, you're probably doing that already.

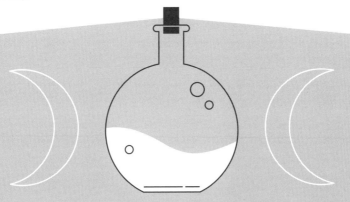

## PRACTICAL MAGIC

Want to infuse your spellwork with even more of the moon's magic? Moon water's the way to go, and it's easy as hell to make. You literally just set your intention and leave water out to be charged by the moon, then use it however you need to. (If you're going to be drinking the water, make sure it has a lid on it while it sits out.) The full moon is the obvious choice because it's complete in its power, but you can charge your water with a particular phase's energy when it's helpful. You can also take into account which zodiac sign the moon is in, if you want to get really focused. The only time you don't want to make moon water? During a lunar eclipse. You don't need those fucking shadows in your life.

### ✦ The Full Moon

Like a white candle or a clear quartz crystal, the full moon is a kickass magical multitasker. It can help you manifest shit more quickly, come up with creative solutions to problems, give your intuition laser focus, and cleanse your damn tools. And that's just to start. This is the most powerful lunar phase, so be careful what you wish for on full-moon days. Set your intentions and watch them pop up all around you like fireflies on a summer night.

Each year has twelve or thirteen full moons, and each moon has its own unique energy (and usually a pretty fun name, like "Beaver Moon"). Plus, those moons are in different zodiac signs, giving them even more specialized energy. So following the lunar calendar closely can give you endless opportunities to get exactly what you want out of your spellwork.

### ✦ The Waning Moon

The waning moon can bring a sense of grounding, release, and closure, easing transitions into the next phase of your life. It might even bring you a little balance, if you ask nicely. Its subsiding light reminds you to rest and surrender to the Universe a little. Fighting for democracy is one thing, but don't fight just to fight.

As the moon darkens and its phases come to a close, it can also take all the negative shit with it. So it's great for working banishing spells *and* doing some inner work to ditch anything unhelpful, like lingering fear or anxiety. Write down anything that isn't serving you, meditate for a minute on getting rid of it, and then burn what you wrote under the waning moon (in a fire-safe space, obviously).

## Your Own Special Days

Magical holidays, seasons, and phases are all important energetic markers that can help you change the world. But the most effective among them are going to be the ones you feel a connection to. That's why you want to tailor the calendar to your coven and include days that are important to you, whether they're witchy or not. Include not just other holidays, but also your goals as a coven.

Want to chant your way through Election Day? Do it. Want to go big on your birthday and manifest the best year of your life? You can do that, too. Hell, you can celebrate Pie Day if it's a high-energy day for you. On the other hand, if Imbolc means fuck-all to you, skip it. By scheduling rituals and celebrations for the days that call to you, you're ensuring that your energy and the energy of the Universe are meeting on the same frequency. And that's how you get shit done.

## WITCH, YOU GOT THIS!

Tapping into the energy that's already swirling around you
is one of the easiest ways to make your magic better,
and all it takes is looking at a fucking calendar.
Understanding the energy each season brings is key.

Learn something about the pagan holidays
Tailor your intention to the energy of the day
Choose specific days to set an intention
Harness the moon's powerful magic
Make some supercharged moon water
Celebrate your own high-vibe days
Rest when the world rests!

Whether you want to celebrate all the witchy holidays and have moon-phase rituals all month, or you want nothing to do with any of this shit, the calendar's still going to have some kind of sway over your magic. So you may as well use it to your advantage!

# PART THREE

# LEARN SOME KICKASS RITUALS

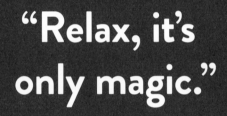

# "Relax, it's only magic."

———— •••• ————

# CHAPTER 10

# GET DOWN TO F\*CKING BUSINESS

**Y**ou made it! This is the fun part, where you get to make magic with your girls. Well, it's almost the fun part. There are a few things you need to know before you dive feet-first into some spellwork. The stuff you do before and after the rituals is just as important as the stuff you do during the rituals. It's just not included *in* the rituals because that would get really fucking repetitive.

Lucky for you, that info's all right here. That doesn't mean you can skip to this section and ignore everything else. (If you have, go back to page 1 right now. You don't want to fuck with magic without having a good foundational understanding of what you're fucking with. Not convinced? Go watch *The Craft*.) Everything you've learned so far, from what to look for in a coven to how to make your own moon water, is about to pay off!

## WTF Even Is a Ritual?

Let's start here: rituals versus spells. You'll usually see rituals as the structure surrounding spells, but they can also be a rite or celebration of their own. For example, you might perform a ritual just to thank your ancestors for having your back. (It's a nice break for them from your constantly asking them for shit.)

And you know a spell when you see one: ingredients lists full of herbs, rhymes that may or may not use the word "mote," instructions for dramatic hand gestures. The thing is, it doesn't have to be that way. "Working a spell" can literally just mean the act of directing your energy toward a desired purpose. And if you're looking for old-timey rhymes, you've come to the wrong book. Here, we're all about tapping into your *own* magic. Getting to choose your words is part of that. Another part is not fucking worrying about the terminology. Spell, ritual, incantation, charm, conjuring, enchantment—nobody gives a shit what you call it. Not even Magic.

## First Things F*cking First

The rituals in this book are pretty fucking clear and use all the stuff you've (hopefully) been reading about. But what you do before working a spell is just as important as what you do while working a spell. Some of these things are necessary for working a spell, like opening the circle, and some are just good suggestions, like wearing yoga pants. All of these things are about supporting your magic, yourself, and your coven. Without that support, your magic might fizzle. Or you could end up burning off your eyebrows because you're not fucking focused on what you're doing. Either way, not great. So read up.

### ✦ Catch Up

The whole point of this book is to help you find your witchy sisters. And sisters dish before they do anything else. Instead of letting yourselves get distracted mid-scrying, spend some time at the beginning of every meeting catching up on shit. Do it over food, and give yourselves enough of a buffer to actually enjoy each other's company without feeling rushed.

Hold space for each other. And make sure you're considerate of everyone's schedules—no one should have to leave mid-ritual because you couldn't make up your mind about appetizers. If you get to the magic, you get to the magic. And if you don't, you'll get 'em next time. Your bond will raise your vibe and fuel your magic. Your meeting agenda will not. Plus, you'll have a chance to work through any energetic blocks that would have fucked with your magic.

### ✦ Power Up

Now that you've gotten a chance to relax with your girls, you can start powering up for your spellwork. First, go over your chosen ritual and make sure you've got everything you need to complete it (including a decent number of brain cells if it's been a long day). You've already started to raise your vibe by relaxing and getting into the right headspace. Now get out of your fucking head and into your body. Dance it out, do some lunges, run around the building five times—whatever. Whether you do cardio or a bit of light stretching, moving your body will help you clear your mind and get your creative energy flowing.

When you're ready, collect everything you need for the ritual you're going to perform. If the ritual (which you have totally read through at least once, right?) says to set your intention before you grab your materials, do that. Make sure you have everything on the list—or at least a good substitution—before you open the circle so that you don't find yourself scrambling.

### ✦ Get Comfy

If you dressed up for your magical pre-gaming, now's the time to change into comfy clothes. (Unless you're one of those covens who go skyclad. Then you do you.) Your energy can only flow if your blood can, and you're about to recalibrate it. Depending on the ritual, it might also be good to wear something you don't mind getting messy. Honey can sweeten a spell, but it can also make stuff stick to your clothes if you spill it.

### ✦ Hunker Down

Start every ritual by doing a grounding exercise. This balances your energy and allows you to focus it on the task at hand. It's a requirement for energy work so you don't feel like you've had your ass kicked afterward, but it's also a great way to shake off the symptoms of unbalanced energy, like headaches, fatigue, forgetfulness, and jumpiness.

There are a ton of ways to ground yourself, and you've probably already used a few at this point: laughing, crying, movement, and food are all on the list. But in order to get into the right energetic space to set an intention, you might want to try something more meditative. Rooting yourself, for example, is a good grounding method.

1. **Stand with your bare feet on the earth (in reasonable temperatures only) and see your energy flowing into the ground like roots.**
2. **Breathe deeply and feel the earth's energy flowing up through those roots and into your body.**
3. **Continue watching the energy flow and cycle like this until you feel good—cool, calm, collected.**

That's it! Now you're ready to make some magic without the magical hangover. (Too bad grounding can't help with an actual hangover.)

## ✦ Create a Sacred Space

For the most part, the space in which you perform a ritual is going to be whatever fucking space you're in. And that's fine. Doing it under the moonlight or in a quiet room is great. Having a dedicated altar is even better. Regardless, you want to cleanse the space before you start. Close your eyes and visualize a white light washing over the space, clearing it of all negative or stagnant energy. You can also use a besom to purify the space, or a mini besom to cleanse an altar.

## ✦ Open the Circle

One way to open your circle is to "call in the quarters," which is a fun way of saying you're going to ask for a little help from the four elements: earth, air, water, and fire. For something like candle magic, you might shove some shit aside on your altar and set up a sort of magical work area. For a larger ritual involving the whole coven, you'd form a physical circle around all of you.

1. **Place representations of the elements at the north, south, east, and west points of a circle around you. For air, you might use feathers. For earth, a bowl of dirt or a rock. Fire can be a candle or incense (unlit is fine), and water can be a literal bowl of water or even a pretty seashell.**

2. In the center, place something to represent your spirituality, like a pentagram or a cross. (Or a pinecone. Or a Jolly Rancher. Whatever speaks to you.)
3. See the items around the circle being connected by a line of energy.
4. Call on the elements one by one, asking for what you want from them. Whatever comes to mind is fine, but it can be something along the lines of, "I call on the element of fire to bring its transformative light."
5. When you're ready, open the circle. You could say something about coming together in the highest expression of love and sisterhood. Or you could say something about coming together to magically kick some bigoted ass. Whatever you want.

Now that the circle is open and the energy is present, it's time for the important shit: intention setting.

## ✧ Set Your Intention

Everything else until now has been the magical equivalent of new-hire paperwork from Human Resources. (A little exciting, but mostly just necessary for you to make it to payday.) This—the setting of your intention—this is the real magic. Spend a little time in meditation to get centered and focus your energy. Let your mind walk around what you want and get a feel for it.

Release any limiting beliefs and tell that monkey mind to take a fucking break. You don't want any unintentional shit ending up in your spellwork, so work on getting super clear about what you want. Visualize the end result and feel it as if it's already happened. Then boil it down to a phrase or a feeling that you can hold onto during the ritual. And it wouldn't be a bad thing for a good witch to add a "with harm to no one" to the end of that intention. It helps ward off any unintentional negativity.

## ✧ Call in the Big Guns

If you want to call on anyone in particular (or even just the Divine Feminine in general) for some spiritual backup, now's the time. You might add a candle to the circle for every god, goddess, or spirit whose help you want with the spell. Make sure you have an offering ready to go. You could offer up your gratitude or your activist intentions for smaller spells, a glass of water for someone you don't call on often, or a shot of whiskey for a bigger ask. But the more you get to know the spirits you call on, the more you come to understand what they like or don't like. (It'll be pretty obvious when your shit works or doesn't work.)

## PRACTICAL MAGIC

Another one of the many magical ways you can ground yourself is with a salt-infused bath (salts have protective properties). This is a good method for when you need a little more grounding than usual, like after a bad news cycle. Add some Dead Sea salt or pink Himalayan salt to a hot bath with some vetiver, sandalwood, and/or cedarwood essential oils—all known for being grounding. Relax into the water, focus on your connection with the Earth through the salt, and let yourself feel cleansed of wonky energy. Bonus points for spending some time in meditation while you soak!

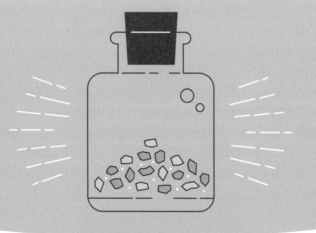

# In the Afterglow

You've done your thing. Now what? Well, you know all the stuff people have been telling you since kindergarten about taking care of yourself? It's even more important when your body is a fucking vessel for magic. After you close the circle, you need to take some time to relax and recharge your batteries. Let go of all the work you just did and trust that the Universe has got it from here. Try to avoid Monday-morning quarterbacking and just enjoy the buzz of energy in the air and each other's company.

### ✦ Closing the Circle

Before you finish up, make sure you thank everyone who came out to help—goddesses, ancestors, and elements included. You want to do this in the oppo-site order to which you called them in, like you're announcing cast members at a curtain call. And no blanket Thank Yous. Address each spirit or source individu-ally and tailor the gratitude to them. It's what Emily Post would do, and it's also what spirits require if you ever want their fucking help again. But then you can (and should) move on with your night. Avoid working more than one spell at a meeting or your energy will be an absolute clusterfuck.

### ✦ Magical Self-Care

Clean everything up right away, both because you don't want any errant energy getting on your tools and because you won't feel like it later. That's just present-you taking care of future-you. Then sit down and take stock of how you're feeling and what your body needs. Make sure you hydrate whether you feel thirsty or not, and maybe grab a snack. Magic is hungry work.

A great way to finish out your meetings is to follow up your spellwork with a chat over wine and charcuterie. (Or beer and pizza. Or tea and doughnuts. What-ever the hell you want. You worked hard. You deserve it.) Check in with each other and talk about next steps, but keep it relaxed and make sure you're not taking on too much. You don't have to change the world in one night!

# Just in F*cking General

By this point, you have everything you need to make amazing, impactful magic together. Everything else is gravy. But it's still tasty, so maybe keep reading anyway. There are a few general tips and tricks that can help ensure your magic is as effective and powerful as possible, like enjoying what you do and keeping that self-confidence as high as your vibe. These may seem like little things, but they can make all the difference.

### ✦ Take It Seriously

If you want to screw around, break out the tarot cards. Yes, they require belief and intention to work properly. They can also be just a bit of fun if you don't care whether they're working properly. But you can't get away with that shit when it comes to spellwork. You have to have some intention behind your actions or it's like lighting a sparkler in the rain—disappointing and a waste of a fucking spark. Make sure you have a good reason for doing any kind of magic, and that you're approaching it with respect. Magic doesn't fuck with people who don't take her seriously.

### ✦ But Also Have Fun

You can't just work spells for funsies, but you can have fun while you're working spells. There's a big difference between the two. One sucks all the useful energy out of the air, and the other fuels it. Make your time together, both as sisters and as a coven, empowering, supportive, and enjoyable. That confidence and joy are going to raise your vibration and supercharge your spellwork.

Yes, you should take magic seriously. Sure, you should bring your A-game. But it's totally OK to have a sense of humor during the ritual. Lightness is healthy. Heaviness creates blocks. If your goddess/ancestors/spirits don't have a sense of humor, then who fucking wants their help?

### ✦ Focus on the Good

When you're charged up, you have to be extra careful with your thoughts, words, and actions. Especially as you get deeper into magical activism and do more

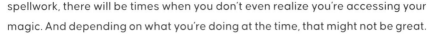

spellwork, there will be times when you don't even realize you're accessing your magic. And depending on what you're doing at the time, that might not be great.

Because your intention focuses your energy, you want to be especially careful there. It should always be framed in a positive way to avoid any bad shit making its way into a spell. So, "The senator will come to his fucking senses and vote for ABC." Not "The senator won't vote for XYZ like an asshole." In other words, think about what you *want* to happen, not what you *don't want* to happen.

## KNOW YOUR SH*T ABOUT GODS

Goddess worship is a pretty standard part of witchcraft. Some witches pray to the God and the Goddess, who represent the duality of all things. Many others pray to the Triple Goddess, who represents different things to different people (like past, present, and future or mother, maiden, and crone). Hecate was one of the early triple goddesses, but she's not the only one. Still, she's a damn helpful deity to have around.

It's OK if you don't believe in the existence of Athena or Hecate as actual beings. You can pray to the idea of them—to the Divine Feminine, for the wisdom and powerful energy—to boost your activism. What you're doing is asking the Universe for help and using the symbolism of these deities to focus your intention. Nothing wrong with that. If it works, great. If it doesn't work, try something (or someone) else!

### ✦ Incorporate Your Coven

Even if a ritual seems like a one-woman job, the other coven members can still support the sister performing it. They can stand in a circle and hold the intention in their minds. They can send supportive energy, even when they're not physically in the same place as the person performing the ritual. They can buy her a burrito so she's not distracted by hunger. Basically, there's no reason not to involve your sisters in most of the spellwork you do. Simply by being there for you, they amplify your energy. If you get stuck, you can turn to them for help. And when you're done, they can force your stubborn ass to take a break and relax. That's what sisters are for.

### ✦ Trust Yo' Self

In this next section, you're going to find all kinds of spells and rituals for all kinds of purposes. The point is to give you a broad selection that you can come back to and adapt for your world-changing needs. Browse through these pages and get to know what's available to you before you settle on a particular ritual. They're divided up into four categories to help you quickly find what you need.

Once you feel comfortable with a style, feel free to add your own magic and adapt the ritual for other purposes. Do a search for flowers, herbs, crystals, and more that meet your needs and swap them in. Change methods and steps. Stop worrying so fucking much and have faith that you know what the hell you're doing. You do. Trust yourself, your intuition, and your magic and you can't go wrong.

# WITCH, YOU GOT THIS!

When you're working a spell from this book or you find one online,
it's going to assume you know what the hell you're doing.
That includes all the magical prep that happens before a ritual,
and all the magical recuperation that happens after.

Raise your vibe

Cleanse the space

Open the circle

Set your intention

Call in some spiritual backup

Show your appreciation

Trust yourself

If you don't know how to ground yourself and open a circle, go back
and read this chapter from the beginning. That shit's important.

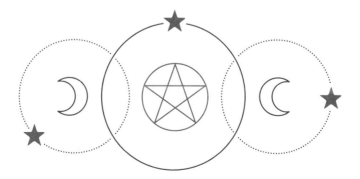

# RITUALS TO GET
## YOU STARTED

This section is full of spellwork to help you start off on the right foot. When you want to raise your vibe, solidify your sisterhood, or manifest something amazing, these are the rituals for you. You'll also find a lovely little confidence booster on pages 120–121 for those days when you're just not feeling it.

# FRESH START
## MOON RITUAL

This easy new-moon ritual is a great way to get to know your girls while dipping your toes into collaborative magic. All you really need is paper, pens, and a new moon. If you want, you can also encourage everyone to bring a crystal that speaks to their intentions. (A few good ones are listed in the Magical Materials below.)

The new moon is the perfect time for starting something, well, new. Your desires and intentions will get caught up in the vortex of hopeful energy that swirls around you while the moon amplifies that excitement and sets you up for success. Use it to bring together a fledgling coven or anytime you need a fresh start for a new intention.

### MAGICAL MATERIALS

Paper

Pens

Rainbow moonstone crystals (for new beginnings)

Amazonite crystals (for hope and success)

Labradorite crystals (for magic and serendipity)

Matches or lighter (optional)

Cauldron or fireproof bowl (optional)

### CLEVER WITCH TIP

Turn your intentions into a sigil using the instructions on page 149 and keep the sigil on you while you work toward manifesting them.

## 1: Pick the Place

Obviously, a new moon is a fucking requirement for a new-moon ritual. Plan accordingly. You can do this ritual anywhere, but doing it outside under the gaze of the dark moon can help you get into it. It also helps with the ventilation should you opt for open flames.

## 2: Set Your Intentions in Writing

Write down what you hope to manifest. How do you want to feel? What do you hope to experience? What do you dream of accomplishing? If you're doing this ritual with your new coven, you might write that you hope to experience sisterhood and growth while ridding your town council of racist bullshit. When adding crystals to the mix, hold them in one hand while you write with the other to amplify your intentions.

## 3: Say It Out Loud

There's a big difference between mulling something over in your head and making a declaration to a group of people who can amplify your inner magic (and help hold you accountable). It's fucking powerful. Have each person read their intentions to the group *with feeling*, infusing the words with kickass world-changing energy. Do it in a superhero pose if you're feeling it.

## 4. Show Your F*cking Support

Now isn't the time for critiques.

Whatever your sister says, clap, cheer, high five, offer words of encouragement—just make sure they feel included, accepted, and fucking magical. If you've done the work of choosing the right witches, you shouldn't get anyone trying to hex their ex or burn politicians at the stake. (If you do, now might be a good time to quietly show them the door and do a quick cleanse.)

## 5: Hand It to the Universe

Once everyone's had their say, either place the papers in your cauldron or fireproof bowl and burn them or tuck them away somewhere safe, where you can come back to them later. The point is to offer your desires to the Universe and let that crafty bitch work out the details.

### MAGICAL MOD

Again, literally anything can be a ritual. If this whole divulging-your-inner-secrets-to-applause is a little too touchy-feely for your taste, skip the circle and go to the diner. Instead of cheering, just talk about your intentions for your work in the coven. The important parts are that you're starting to put out into the world the things you want to accomplish, and that you're supportive of each other's efforts. Do this on the night of a new moon to start your adventure on the right foot.

# BETTER TOGETHER
# COOPERATIVE MAGIC RITUAL

Finally! A magical use for those kickass hair-braiding skills you've been working on since you were five. You knew those would pay off eventually.

Whether you're new to cooperative magic or your coven's shared energy needs a tune-up, this easy cord-braiding ritual can help. It'll strengthen your bonds, open the lines of communication, and make working magic together a much smoother experience.

Your braid doesn't have to be perfect. Hell, it doesn't even have to be pretty. The point is that the strands come together to form something bigger than themselves.

## MAGICAL MATERIALS

Pink candle

Matches or lighter

4 (12-inch) pieces of cord

Scissors

Rose quartz crystal(s)

### CLEVER WITCH TIP

If you're handy with the macramé, you can make whatever you like, infuse it with the same intentions, and have a cool art piece for your covenstead.

## 1. Set the Stage

Holding your intention to forge or strengthen relationships in your mind and the quartz crystal in your nondominant hand, light the candle. If you have a single crystal, place it next to the candle. If you have crystals for each member, place yours by the candle and have everyone clasp a crystal between their hands while sending loving energy to you.

## 2. Sort Out Your Cords

Take three pieces of the cord in your hands and straighten them out on your workspace (watch the candle—this ritual does not involve setting shit on fire). Then cut the remaining piece in half and tie one half around all three at their center. That piece is Magic, effortlessly holding shit together.

## 3. Get to Braiding

Bring the cords down on either side of the knot to line up with each other. You should have three strands on the left and three strands on the right. Carefully lift the far-right strand over the one next to it and under the one next to that until it's in the center. Do the same on the other side, finally weaving the strand under the one in the center. Keep going until there's nothing left to braid. (You can do this on your work surface or in your hands, depending on whether you have ninja-like braiding skills or no idea what the fuck you're doing.)

## 4. Meditate on Your Intention

Use the last bit of cord to tie a knot around the bottom of the braid, sealing in your intentions. Lay the braid next to your candle and crystal and settle in to meditate for a while. See your coven's unity, collaboration, communication, and cooperative magic not just improving, but becoming effortless.

## 5. Honor the Braid's Message

Hang the braid in a place of honor by your shared altar. Alternatively, you could take a page out of your local knitting club's book and have each member create their own braid. Then each could have a braid as a reminder of your shared magic, and how much fucking stronger it is when you work it together.

### MAGICAL MOD

Just being together in the circle should infuse the ritual with enough cooperative energy. But if you want to go all "Scouts at summer camp" about it, you can each have a hand in the actual braiding. Take turns, with each sister braiding the next strand, until you reach the end. Then finish things off by toasting marshmallows over the candle. (Not really. But you totally could. It can't hurt.)

# QUICK-HIT CHAKRA BALANCING RITUAL

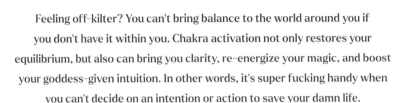

Feeling off-kilter? You can't bring balance to the world around you if you don't have it within you. Chakra activation not only restores your equilibrium, but also can bring you clarity, re-energize your magic, and boost your goddess-given intuition. In other words, it's super fucking handy when you can't decide on an intention or action to save your damn life.

This one is best done during a full moon, which helps you ditch all the negative chakra-blocking bullshit before the new moon comes calling with all it's new-adventure energy. It's a simple visualization, so all you really need is you. But a little amplification never hurts.

## MAGICAL MATERIALS

Lavender oil

Clear quartz crystals

Badass visualization skills

### CLEVER WITCH TIP

If you're not familiar with chakras, do yourself a favor and look them up. Knowing where they're located and what the symptoms of imbalance are can be a fucking lifesaver.

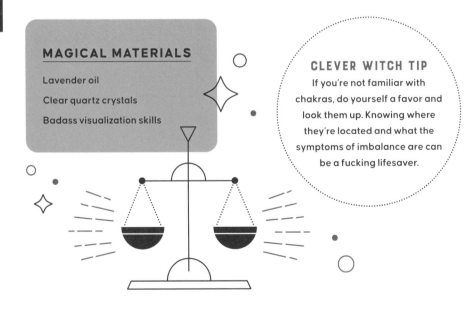

## 1: Get into Position

Choose a spot where you can see the full moon. This not only helps the moon charge your intentions but also helps anchor the visualization.

## 2: Activate Your Third Eye

Dab a bit of the lavender oil on your Third Eye Chakra between your eyebrows. (Don't worry—it's safe for even sensitive skin. Just don't get it in your fucking eyes.)

## 3: Lasso the Moon('s Energy)

Holding a quartz crystal in your hands, visualize it absorbing the light of the moon. Feel the tingling sensation in your hands. Then see the energy of each chakra (represented by its color) being pulled into the crystal like you're Ron Weasley holding the Deluminator.

## 4: Bring 'Em Back

Visualize the energy coming back to you recharged, one chakra at a time, and feel its effects. The red energy of the Root Chakra hits the base of your spine and makes you feel grounded. You see the orange of the Sacral Chakra circling your naval and feel creative and confident. The yellow of the Solar Plexus Chakra leaves the crystal, enters your stomach, and fills you with strength. Warm, green energy enters your heart and makes you feel joy and peace. See how the blue energy of the Throat Chakra lets your words and truth flow freely. The Third Eye Chakra's indigo energy awakens your intuition. And finally, purple energy enters the Crown Chakra at the top of your head and connects you to your highest self.

## 5: Feel Your Feelings

Feel the energy buzzing through your whole body. See the colors of the chakras aligned with white lunar light. With all your chakras recharged by the moon, you should feel energized, excited, and most of all, balanced.

## 6: Release the Moon

See the connection between the moon and the crystal break and the white energy travel back up to the moon. Take one last deep breath as you offer your thanks to the moon.

### MAGICAL MOD

This ritual is a quick hit for a full chakra rebalancing. But if you know which chakra is giving you issues, you can target it directly. A quick search will tell you the crystals and oils to use to release a specific block. For example, if you need to awaken your third eye, meditate on it with lemon oil diffusing and amethyst, labradorite, or lapis lazuli in hand.

# MANIFESTATION  IN A FLASH RITUAL

Yes, you are serious witches up against serious world issues.
And yes, magic is some serious shit. But that doesn't mean you can't have
a little magic-show-style fun every now and then. Flash paper adds a little
extra zhuzh to the otherwise pretty uneventful act of manifesting intentions.

To be clear, the flash in this ritual refers to the paper, not the timing. That
shit takes as long as it takes. But you can help it along by not giving it another
thought. Yep—you read that right. Let Magic take the wheel on this one.

## MAGICAL MATERIALS

Flash paper

Pens or markers

Matches or lighter

Cauldron or fireproof bowl

Crystals (optional)

Candles (optional)

### CLEVER WITCH TIP

Give your ritual a boost with
a few crystals and candles
specifically attuned to your
intention. Quartz crystals and
white candles will do in a pinch!

### 1: Talk It Out

When working as a coven, it's pretty damn important that everyone be on the same page with their intentions. Have a discussion about what you want to accomplish *before* you open the circle. Pick an intention you can all get behind and get super fucking specific about it. For example, "We want to manifest the courage and badass communication skills to convince Senator Michaels to vote for the climate-crisis bill tomorrow."

### 2: Write It Down

Grab your flash paper and pens and write down what you want to manifest. You have three options: 1) Everyone writes the same thing on their paper to amplify the intention. 2) Everyone writes down a different small component of the same larger intention—like breaking down the steps needed to accomplish a goal. 3) Everyone writes down the thing they, themselves, need to get the job done (courage, money, time, a clone—whatever.)

### 3: Take It In

Take a moment to internalize your chosen intention and infuse it with your energy. See it coming true in your mind's eye. Holding an amplifying crystal in one hand and the paper in the other can help with this.

### 4: Light It Up

When you're ready, use a match, lighter, or lit candle to set the corner of the paper on fire. The paper should burn away to nothing, but better safe than setting your house on fire. Hold the paper over your cauldron, fire-safe bowl, or even a fire pit while you light it.

### 5: Let It Go

Once you light the fire, it's time to let that shit go—literally. This part takes a little finesse and a lot of paying fucking attention. When the flame gets close to your fingers, Let. Go. Don't wait until the damn thing burns you, but also don't let go so early that the flame has a chance to hit something else before it goes out. When you're done, it's time to let the intention go, too, and trust that what you want is on its way to you.

> **MAGICAL MOD**
>
> Flash paper is fun, but it's not necessary. Any scrap of paper will do. But you're literally playing with fucking fire here, so make sure you observe fire safety. In other words, don't do this ritual in the woods surrounded by fucking kindling. Flash paper will burn up in an instant without leaving any ash. Regular paper needs to be burned in—not just over—a fireproof receptacle. Don't worry, though. Both are effective and satisfying AF.

# CONFIDENCE-BOOSTING
## ◇◇ MIRROR RITUAL ◇◇

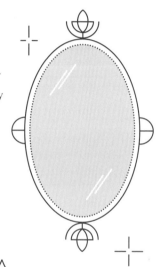

There's a reason that saying affirmations into a mirror is so effective. Consciously or not, we infuse our words with our energy. And being face to face with ourselves ensures that we really hear those words—not least of all because we're usually pretty fucking self-conscious about doing it.

But let's be real—you talk to yourself all the time. Everyone does. And when you do it with intention, it gets the fucking job done. So let's all just get over ourselves and stop feeling so damn silly about it. The confidence it inspires can help you change the fucking world.

## MAGICAL MATERIALS

A small purple or yellow candle

Essential oils like cedarwood, ylang-ylang, jasmine, bergamot, or orange

Full-length mirror

Pen

Paper

### CLEVER WITCH TIP

Buy an essential-oil roller filled with a confidence-boosting blend to use for rituals like this one—or just to huff before doing something brave.

### 1: Set Aside Some Time

You need at least 15 uninterrupted minutes to devote to this—no notifications, no appointments to get to, nothing. This may feel more like self-help than magic, but it still requires your full attention.

### 2: Get Your Chakras Involved

Sit in front of the mirror and breathe deeply into your diaphragm (otherwise known as the Solar Plexus Chakra, which has dibs on your confidence levels). Then light the candle.

### 3: Pen a Memoir of Badassery

Using the pen and paper, write down all the things about you that are amazing, from your homemade cobbler to your desire to change the fucking world. If you're having trouble with this because modesty is deeply ingrained in you from years of social conditioning, write from the perspective of your best friend. Or just channel Margo from *The Magicians*. Allow yourself to really feel each accomplishment and quality as you write it.

### 4: Prepare Some Affirmations

When you're done, take a minute to reread everything and meditate on (read: bask in) your awesomeness. Then pick out a few facts to use as affirmations, like, "I am a badass magical activist who is going to change the fucking world." Choose affirmations that speak directly to your needs, either to shore up some confidence for an upcoming event or to bolster areas where your energy feels weak.

### 5: Finish Strong

Anoint your forehead, wrists, and neck with your favorite essential oils (safely mixed with a carrier oil). Then, while staring deeply into your own eyes, say your affirmations. Allow the candle to finish burning, then go about your day as the badass you were born to be.

### 6: Keep the Magic Going

Don't even think about shredding that paper. Instead, tuck it under your pillow. Repeat the affirmations every morning and night for at least a full week or as long as you need to feel imbued with its magic.

> **MAGICAL MOD**
>
> Adapt this ritual for a coven by letting the members act as a mirror. Focusing on one member at a time, have everyone offer up something they love or admire about that person. (Eye contact is a must for this.) After each confidence booster, the recipient should repeat the compliment as an affirmation. Seal in the magic with applause and cheers, then move onto the next member. This is an incredibly powerful ritual to perform the night before a big push or event.

# RITUALS TO
## FOCUS UP

Distractions happen, but Magic doesn't love a
scatterbrained spellworker. When you're a little
stopped up (magically speaking), having trouble
hunkering down, feeling uninspired, or just need to
clear the air, you can turn to these rituals. And as
a bonus, this section includes a couple ways to tap
into that all-powerful intuition of yours.

RITUAL

# FIFTEEN-MINUTE FOCUS
## — INCENSE RITUAL —

This quick and simple incense ritual is your chance to hit the reset button and to get your head on straight. It's especially handy if you end up in a shouting match with your sisters over the best way to approach a problem, but it also works well when you've just gotten off track. Shut it down, light it up, and sit quietly for a while like you're in an energetic timeout.

When you do that, you give all those competing thoughts and opinions time to simmer. Then you get to see what floats to the top. Plus, you'll be super fucking mellow and clearheaded after those 15 minutes of quiet focus.

## MAGICAL MATERIALS

Cinnamon incense

Incense holder

Matches or lighter

Crystals like:

Blue quartz (clarity)

Fluorite (focus)

Black tourmaline (protection from negativity)

Malachite (letting go)

Amazonite (communication)

Pens

Paper

### CLEVER WITCH TIP
If you don't have cinnamon incense lying around but do have a heavily scented cinnamon candle leftover from winter, don't think twice about swapping that baby in.

124

### 1: Hit the Pause Button

When you feel things getting unproductive—whether that's due to a fight, a food coma, or just a general lack of attention span—shut it down. Move the party to a quiet space without distractions and crack a window to literally clear the air.

### 2: Get Clear on Your Intention

Once you're grounded and ready to start the ritual, you're already in a way better headspace. Now you can discuss your shared intention. But for no more than a minute—the point is not to start another fucking debate. Something like, "We will find focus and clarity in our time together" will do, but you can get more specific if you've got a meeting agenda to adhere to.

### 3: Add Some Sparkle

If crystals are your thing, you can infuse this ritual with their energy in one of two ways: 1) have members hold them throughout, or 2) place them in a circle around your incense burner and let the smoke wash over them. Either way will leave your crystals with a bit of that focused energy.

### 4: Focus the F*ck Up

The mindfulness starts now. Light the incense in the center of your circle. As the flame goes out, focus on the smoke. Fully immerse yourself in its movements. If you feel like it, you can close your eyes and focus on its spicy, inspiring scent. Let any thoughts come and go, always bringing your attention back to the incense, until the smoke clears. (For most incense, that should be about 15 minutes. But you also can set a timer.)

### 5: Write It Down

Before anyone speaks, take a few minutes to free-write. Start with how you're feeling, then see if anything else comes to the surface. With your brain clear and focused, you might be surprised at what new perspectives present themselves.

### 6: Have a Conversation

Now that everyone's refreshed and focused, take turns sharing your thoughts. Keep that calm, focused energy intact by hearing everyone out completely before discussing what they've shared. Then toast to your creative breakthroughs!

> **MAGICAL MOD**
>
> You can also use this ritual for manifestation by swapping out the incense for a scent that speaks to your intention. Jasmine and rose can open up the heart chakra, lavender can keep anxiety at bay, and bergamot can help you gear up for a fight with courage and confidence. And that's just the tip of the very fragrant iceberg!

# BLOCK-BUSTING
## TEA RITUAL

Whether a block is physical, mental, emotional, or energetic, it's fucking annoying. And it's really going to put a damper on this whole saving-the-world thing. Luckily, there's an easy—and rather delightful—ritual for this one.

Instead of a cauldron, you're going to brew this potion in your favorite teacup or mug. The ingredients help you focus, the sipping clears your mind, and the magic shifts that annoying shit out of your way. Just leave yourself a little extra time in the morning to enjoy a quiet cup or two without interruption. This is an enjoyable ritual, but it still requires your full attention.

## MAGICAL MATERIALS

Smallish amethyst crystal

Drinkable water

Kettle

Tealight candle

Lavender oil

Peppermint tea

Honey

Slice of lemon

Pen

Paper

### CLEVER WITCH TIP

Add your amethyst crystal to water charged by the waxing crescent moon for a boost of wisdom, positivity, and block-busting energy.

## 1: Charge Your Tea Water

Drop your (clean and cleansed) amethyst crystal into a bottle, jar, or whatever receptacle you have that will hold 16 ounces of water. Go to sleep and let the amethyst do its thing overnight.

## 2: Set the Magical Mood

Pour the amethyst water (but not the amethyst) into a kettle and let it come to a boil while you get everything ready. Anoint the tealight with the lavender oil by putting some on the tip of your finger and dragging it over the top of the candle around the wick (counterclockwise when you want to banish bad shit like blocks).

## 3: Steep Your Tea

When the water is ready, light the candle and begin setting your intention to break through any mental, physical, emotional, or energetic blocks and come out on the other side clear-headed and ready for fucking anything. Infuse your actions with that intention as you add your tea bag (or infuser, if you're fancy) to your favorite mug and pour the hot water over it.

## 4: Sweeten the Pot

Breathe in the peppermint, which stimulates the mind. Stir in honey to sweeten the outcome of the spell and a squeeze of lemon juice to brighten it. (The citrus zing combined with the peppermint also helps your brain focus.)

## 5: Get to F*cking Work

Time to break out that pen and paper. Have a seat and sip your tea while you envision the kickass stuff you want to accomplish. Write it out in whatever form works for you—list, narrative, dirty limerick. When you're done, fold the paper in half toward you. Seal that shit by drawing on it a sigil or symbol that says "flow" to you. (Overthinking this would be fucking counterproductive. You can always just write the word "flow.")

## 6: Finish Your Tea

Sip your tea like Kermit while you wait for the candle to burn out and think about how awesome life will be without all those annoying blocks. Then carry on with your fucking day and forget about it. The hardest (and most crucial) part of this spell is just having faith that it worked and the right path will present itself.

### MAGICAL MOD

No stove? Nary a kettle in sight? This is the 21st century, and Magic fucking knows it. Microwaving your tea water isn't going to hurt anything or make the ritual any less effective. The magic is in you—not your mug. Microwaving your amethyst crystal, however, is probably not a great idea. Make sure you don't dump it into your mug in a block-related brain fog.

# AIR-CLEARING COMMUNICATIONS RITUAL

▽

Put any two people in a room often enough and you're sure to have a misunderstanding now and then. Put a bunch of badass magical activists in a room together and you're going to have some *opinions*. The important thing is to learn how to hear each other out and to put any disagreements (or all-out arguments) behind you so you can brunch the next day with a clear mind and strong stomach.

If the conversation's an important one to have, this ritual can make it more productive. If it's not, the ritual will help you realize that and move the hell on. But you can also use these steps to release negative thoughts or habits that no longer serve you, from self-destructive behavior to stale beliefs. So give yourself the fresh start you fucking deserve.

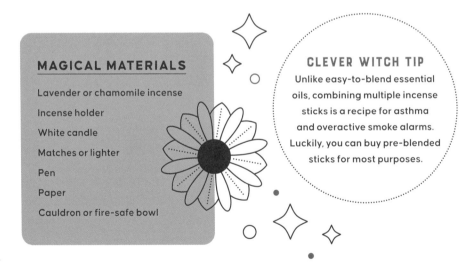

## MAGICAL MATERIALS

Lavender or chamomile incense

Incense holder

White candle

Matches or lighter

Pen

Paper

Cauldron or fire-safe bowl

### CLEVER WITCH TIP

Unlike easy-to-blend essential oils, combining multiple incense sticks is a recipe for asthma and overactive smoke alarms. Luckily, you can buy pre-blended sticks for most purposes.

### 1: Cleanse Your Space

You don't need the energy in the space adding to your problems. (For all you know, that's what fucking started them.) Whether you use the cleansing ritual on page 72, spritz some rosewater around the place, or swish it away using a besom, get it done before you start.

### 2: Set Your Intention Alight

Once you're all grounded and ready, place the incense, candle, and cauldron in the center of your circle. Light the incense and the candle and focus your mind on your intentions. Note: your intention here shouldn't be, "To have these bitches realize I'm right." Your intention should be along the lines of, "To clear the air, have some fucking empathy, and start fresh so that we can have a productive conversation."

### 3: Have a Healthy Little Vent Sesh

Using the pen and paper, spend a few minutes getting it all out—what you think about everything, what's pissing you off, all of it. Then spend a few more minutes writing about why you want to clear the air (e.g., because you love your girls and you can't change the world together while tiptoeing around the feelings you hurt).

### 4: Cleanse Your Thoughts

When you're done, fold your paper in half like you're closing the book on that shit. Then, one at a time, pass your papers back and forth over the smoke of the incense three times while visualizing the tension dissolving. You can say a little spell or prayer of your own devising while doing this, if you want.

### 5: F*cking Let It Go

When you're finished with the cleansing, use the candle's flame to light the corner of the paper on fire and drop the paper into your cauldron. This is you letting go of all that close-mindedness and negativity. You can say it out loud if you want—something like, "I release all the bad shit and vow to start fresh with an open mind." Then follow through.

> **MAGICAL MOD**
>
> Before you dive into the ritual, charge a piece of lapis lazuli (the "stone of truth") for a positive outcome. Hold it in your hand and see yourself post-exchange feeling relieved and satisfied with how things went. Feel this positivity and self-confidence flowing into the stone, charging it up. Then keep the stone nearby to help you communicate more clearly (and avoid the whole foot-in-mouth thing) once you've cleared the air. This is a great ritual of its own to perform anytime you're nervous about meeting with someone, like your local reps.

RITUAL

# MAGICAL MUSE
## ⟩ MOON-SCRYING RITUAL ⟨

By necessity, witches are some of the most creative bitches on the planet. You can't do what we do without stepping outside the box and putting your fucking mind to work. But as humans, we're not always feeling it when we need to. Of course, you can't run out of creativity. The more you use it, the more you have. That doesn't mean it won't occasionally disappear on you like a damn two-dollar lip balm.

This ritual taps into the moon's unending magic on those days when you need some inspiration. (It can't help you with your lip balm, though. Not even a psychic can help you find those fuckers.) Use it whenever you need to get those creative juices flowing, like when you're deciding on your next collab or trying to solve a particularly hairy problem.

### MAGICAL MATERIALS

Cauldron or dark-colored bowl

Water

Food coloring

Toothpick or spoon

Pen

Paper

Creative crystals (optional)

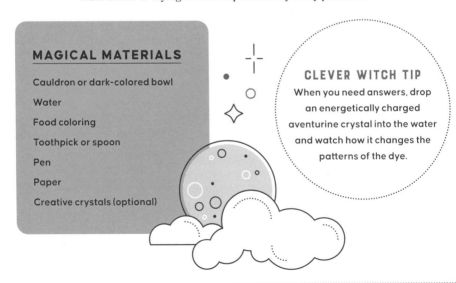

### CLEVER WITCH TIP
When you need answers, drop an energetically charged aventurine crystal into the water and watch how it changes the patterns of the dye.

## 1: Wait for the Fullest Moon

Because you're tapping into the moon's creative energy, you'll want to do this ritual when the moon is fullest. Fill a cauldron or dark bowl with water, take it outside, and put it wherever it can easily reflect the moon. (If you set up a circle beforehand, use a mirror to see where the bowl will go. But be quick about it—the planet isn't going to stop fucking turning for you.)

## 2: Clear Your Creative Blocks

With your pen and paper handy, sit close to the bowl so that you can look straight down into the water. When doing this with a coven, you can stand shoulder-to-shoulder—or just take turns peering into the water. Either way, close your eyes and feel the moon's light wash over you, cleansing you of creativity-killing energy blocks.

## 3: Set Your Intention

When you feel ready, bring your intention to mind. This can be a general, "Let the brilliant energy of the moon inspire in me great ideas," or a more specific, "Let the brilliant energy of the moon clear out my fucking brain fog so I can come up with a way to get my pig-headed brother to see reason."

## 4: Add Some Color

Trust the moon to have the answers—no matter what the question—as you add a drop or two of food coloring to the water. (Give it a quick swirl if it doesn't automatically expand. The moon can't do everything for you.) The color should move through the water and take shape like thoughts in your mind.

## 5: Take Note

Let the water come in and out of focus until you find what feels good, then spend some time with it. Write down anything the movement, patterns, and shapes inspire in you. This isn't like tea leaves—you're going to be hard-fucking-pressed to find a clearly shaped dog or crescent moon. This is more like seeing a dog in the clouds where your friend sees an apricot. What you see is what's meant for you. Take it and run with it!

### MAGICAL MOD

Guess what! The moon is always there, whether you see it or not. So no need to stand outside in the dark like a fucking vampire for every spell that taps into its energy. For this one, you need just enough light to be able to see the water but enough darkness to cast shadows. Use a large white candle for the light and visualize the moon's energy flooding in and filling the space before you set your intention.

# A HOT CUP OF
# CLARI-TEA

Making a difference starts with getting clear on what you want to achieve. Easier said than done, right? This tea ritual can calm that monkey mind and help you figure out what's really important to you.

You can whip up a cup anytime you need it, but a new moon can infuse the tea with some much-needed clean-slate energy. Have some before bedtime and let its magic help you wake up with a clear head. Of course, if it's not clarity you need but an energetic bulldozer for those blocks you're carrying around, check out the other tea recipe on page 126.

carrying around, check out the other tea recipe on page 126.

## MAGICAL MATERIALS

Drinkable water

Kettle

Spoon

Dried mugwort

Dried chamomile

Dried lavender

Dried valerian

Dried cinnamon

Small bowl

Loose leaf tea infuser

Favorite teacup or mug

Honey (optional)

**CLEVER WITCH TIP**

Charge some bottles of water under the new moon so you have them at the ready for rituals like this one. Just remember to label the damn things.

### 1: Clean Sh*t Up

Before you start, make sure your space is clean. This isn't about the dirty dishes in the sink. (But would it kill you to load the dishwasher?) It's about starting with fresh energy. Whether you do a quick visualization or a full-out cleansing, clear out any unhelpful shit.

### 2: Set Your Intention

Add some water to your kettle and bring it to a boil while you set your intention. "To make sense of my own fucking thoughts" is a good one. But you can go a little more old-school witchy with something like, "With this tea / let me see / that which is / meant for me." Do you.

### 3: Prep the Tea

Use a spoon to combine half a teaspoon of each herb in a small bowl, then to fill your tea infuser with the mindful mixture. Place the infuser in your favorite cup and pour the boiling water over it.

### 4: Let Everything Steep—Including You

Let the herbs steep for up to 10 minutes while you meditate on your intention, breathing the flowery scent into your Solar Plexus Chakra (a.k.a. the diaphragm). Bringing balance to this chakra can give you the confidence you need to make good choices.

### 5: Sweeten the Pot

Remove the infuser and use the same spoon to stir your tea clockwise (to bring clarity to you), infusing it with your intention and some badass decision-making energy. Not a fan of unsweetened tea? No problem. Stir in a little honey not only to bring out the flavors in the tea but also to ensure a sweet outcome for the spell.

### 6: Get Out of Your Damn Head

Sip the tea and feel the warmth of its clarifying energy spreading through you. Try to let your thoughts continue to come and go without attaching to any of them. Giving your brain time to rest while the tea goes to work can mean some brilliant fucking breakthroughs later.

> **MAGICAL MOD**
>
> If you'd rather drink a cup of literal dirt than a cup of herbal tea (hey, it's not for everyone), you can still find some sanity using this ritual. Turn the herbs into potpourri by letting them simmer in a pot of water while you infuse your morning cup of coffee with the same intention. And if you're just too lazy or don't want to spend your paycheck on all these herbs, find yourself a pre-blended tea for the purpose. There's no fucking shortage.

# A VERY
# THIRD-EYE-OPENING

# RITUAL

Your intuition is your birthright, not just as a witch but also as one of billions of human beings sharing a collective consciousness on this crazy planet. With practice, meditation, and, of course, a little magic, you can tap into that universal knowledge whenever the hell you want to.

This intuition-boosting ritual is part charm bag, part crystal grid, and all fucking powerful at charging up those natural abilities. Will you be able to hear your girlfriend's thoughts? No. (That's for the best.) But will you be able to make good, informed decisions? Yes. (And that's best for everyone, too.)

## MAGICAL MATERIALS

White candle

Silver candle

Purple candle

Lavender or rosemary essential oil

Dried lavender or rosemary

Purple tourmaline crystal

Moonstone crystal

Moss agate crystal

Jet crystal

Blue topaz crystal

Blue or white pouch

### CLEVER WITCH TIP
Say a little prayer to Hecate over your charm bag. As the Triple Goddess, she's also the goddess of intuitive and psychic wisdom.

### 1: Anoint Your Candles

Holding your intention in your mind, anoint each candle: Dip your fingers in the essential oil and gently drag them along the wax from top to middle and then bottom to middle, symbolically bringing intuition to you.

### 2: Create Your Crystal-Candle Grid

Continue to hold your intention in your mind as you place the pouch in the center of the circle and sprinkle the lavender or rosemary over it. Put the purple candle to the left of the pouch, then the tourmaline above the candle. Next, put the white candle to the right of the pouch and the moonstone above that candle. Finally, put the silver candle below the pouch and the jet below that.

### 3: Open That Third Eye

Connect the purple and silver candles by placing the agate in between them and connect the white and silver candles by placing the topaz between them. Then meditate on their intuition-boosting energy, visualizing your Third Eye Chakra being charged by it. See the blocks being cleared away and feel the clarity and joy of knowing exactly what to do next.

### 4: Listen the F*ck Up

Once you're filled with that radiant, positive energy, say your intention (or a spell of your own design) out loud. Then sit in quiet meditation for at least 10 minutes, doing absolutely fucking nothing but listening for the Universe to speak.

### 5: Create and Keep Your Charm Bag

Allow the candles to burn out completely, then sweep your dried herbs and crystals into the pouch. Close it and either carry it with you or keep it on your altar, remembering to recharge it once in a while. Every so often, sit in meditation with the pouch nearby and listen. Intuition is like a muscle. And as fucking annoying as it can be to work our muscles, it can only make us better.

> **MAGICAL MOD**
>
> Don't have a whole bunch of crystals and different-colored candles just lying around? Don't worry about it. While all those extras can help amplify your intention, the important part is turning inward. Light a candle with a lovely, calming scent, close your eyes, and visualize energetic blocks being thrown open by a bright, white light. Once they're gone, sit quietly and listen. The more often you do this, the more easily the information will come to you. (Use a snuffer when you're done. Why waste a good scented candle?)

# RITUALS TO
## GET SH*T DONE

Ready to get to fucking work? From healing
rituals and persuasion magic to protective sigils
and spellwork for social justice, this section has
everything the magical activist needs to change the
world. There's even a ritual for banishing bullshit!
Save the rituals in this section for when you're up
on your magic and really feeling yourself.

# LOW-AND-SLOW CANDLE MANIFESTATION RITUAL

When you run into a big-ass problem, you need some
sustained magic to help you break it down. Let this seven-day
candle ritual go to work while you focus your energy elsewhere.

A seven-day candle is just a pillar candle with enough wax to burn for seven days. So that you don't start yet another uncontrollable wildfire, you're going to light it for a few minutes each day. The point is just to let the spell simmer for a while and infuse your intention with more magical flavor. When working this spell with a coven, everyone should have their own candle. Whether they also have their own intentions is up to you.

The items listed below are like your basic manifestation kit for making shit happen. But you can DIY the hell out of this ritual by swapping out the candle color, essential oil, and herbs to create a powerful combo for your specific intention. Want world peace? Combine a light blue candle (peace) with eucalyptus oil (healing) and dried roses (love) to bridge the divide between two sides. You get the idea.

## MAGICAL MATERIALS

A white seven-day candle

Lavender essential oil

Dried rosemary

Mortar and pestle

Candle snuffer

VII

### CLEVER WITCH TIP

Do a quick search on sites like Etsy, and you'll find a bunch of candles for sale that are already blended and blessed for your desired purpose.

### 1: Get in the Right Headspace

Carve out a good 15 minutes for this ritual. You're going to start like you always do, with grounding and clearing your mind to make way for magic. Get centered using your breath.

### 2: Set Your Intention

Place the unlit candle in front of you and hold your intention in your mind. See it coming to fruition and feel how that feels. Let everything you do from this moment be infused with that energy.

### 3: Amp Up the Magic

Use the mortar and pestle to grind the rosemary and sprinkle it around the wick. (Don't go crazy with it. You don't want to create a fucking fire hazard.) Add a drop or two of the lavender oil to the top of the candle. Then hold the candle in both hands and charge it with your intention.

### 4: Finally Light the Damn Candle

Once you're sure you've infused your candle with your intention, set it down and light it up. You can sit in quiet meditation for a few minutes or talk to your girls about next steps. Either way, you want to let the candle burn for a bit. When you're done, use a snuffer to put out the candle (don't blow on it—that's a whole other kind of magic) and close the circle. Note: Always make sure you're in a safe area and paying attention before messing with fire, even if it's just a fucking candle.

### 5: Do It All Again (Or Not)

The point of this ritual is to keep it going over time. That could be every day for a week (or until the candle burns out), once a week, or once a month for big, ambitious, long-term goals. Some witches do the whole ritual every time they light the candle. Others trust that infusing it once will get the job done. You do you, but you should at least take a moment to focus on your intention each time you light the wick.

## MAGICAL MOD

This is a ritual you can do anywhere in a pinch. Skip the oils and herbs and grab a prayer candle from the nearest convenience store. If you want a magical boost, you can buy a cheap pocketknife, bless it, and (very fucking carefully) carve a sigil or symbol into the wax. Just don't go lighting candles in your motel room—those linens are cheap AF and *will* go up in flames. And managers tend to frown on guests who set the fucking place on fire.

# REMOTE
# HEALING RITUAL

If you've always wanted to try reiki, this is the ritual for you. This ancient art has endless benefits, including relaxation and healing. And if you think that reiki is some woo-woo New Age bullshit they offer at spas to upcharge clients, it's time to broaden your magical horizons. Tapping into your magic to support others is what witches do.

Reiki is often performed up close and personal with the recipient. But it's also a simple yet powerful thing to do when you're feeling helpless hundreds of miles away from someone in need of support. You can send healing energy to a single person or an entire group of people—no matter where they are. Those protestors three states away? That victim of assault who's bravely coming forward on the six o'clock news? With this ritual, you can have their fucking backs.

## MAGICAL MATERIALS

Gratitude

Crystals like:

   Turquoise (healing)

   Rose quartz (love)

   Smokey quartz (protection)

   Carnelian (inspiration)

A picture of the recipient

Pen

Paper

### CLEVER WITCH TIP
You may never know whether your healing energy reaches its intended recipient, or whether they choose to receive it. Having faith that it will is the only way that it can.

### 1: First Things First

Start things off with a quick mental cleansing, closing your eyes and scanning your body for any sticking points. Send white, cleansing energy through those points.

### 2: Find Your Happy Place

Now that you've cleared the blocks, you have to clear out any lingering negativity (i.e., get happy). Practice a few minutes of joyful gratitude to bring up your vibe.

### 3: Dip into the Universe's Reserves

You can work some spells with the energy you have in your little finger. This is not one of them. Once things are flowing, you're going to tap into the magic of the Universe. See yourself connecting with the healing energy swirling around you. Feel it coursing through your body, peaceful yet powerful. Holding onto one or more of the crystals listed can help infuse that energy with your intention.

### 4: Work Smarter, Not Harder

Can you just use your imagination? Absolutely. But it'll be a hell of a lot easier to direct your energy if you're looking at a picture of your recipient. (If you can Facetime them, even better!)

### 5: Hug It Out (Energetically Speaking)

Visualize sending the energy to them and seeing them wrapped up in its healing glow. Some reiki practitioners swear by the long-distance healing symbol. If you want to incorporate it, draw the symbol with your hand in the air while holding onto your energetic connection. Alternatively, you can write the recipient's name and the symbol on a piece of paper, fold it, hold it, and send energy to it.

### 6: Spend Some Time on It

This ritual is worth doing even if you only have a few minutes to spare. Generally speaking, the more time you can devote to it, the more healing, supportive energy your recipient will get. Only have 5 minutes? Make it fucking count by flooding your recipient with joyful, radiant energy.

---

**MAGICAL MOD**

Reiki is one of those things that can't hurt and might help, so it's always worthwhile. But, much like DM'ing a crush, it's more effective if the recipient is in on the energy exchange from the beginning. That means it's an awesome thing to do for friends and loved ones who need some support. The only difference is that you ask their permission to perform the ritual on them. The more open they are to receiving that healing energy, the more they'll benefit from it.

# PERSUASIVE AF GLAMOUR SACHET

Old-school glamour spells were used to "help" a person see what you wanted them to see, usually in the service of love (or lust). Even with good intentions, they sort of walk an ethical line. So consider this more of a communication ritual with the va-va-voom of a glamour.

We're not out to fleece anyone here. This ritual is really about ensuring that your gift of gab goes unchecked by blocked chakras, toxic energy, or crises of confidence. It'll help you step into your persuasive power while clearing the energetic channels of communication so that you can change some fucking hearts and minds.

## MAGICAL MATERIALS

A mirror that can lie flat

Pen

Paper

A purple candle

Printed photo of yourself

Fresh carnation petals

Blue chamomile essential oil

Frankincense essential oil

Cinnamon

Brown sugar

Matches or lighter

Red sachet or pouch

### CLEVER WITCH TIP

When you don't have the time or fucking patience to wait for a candle to burn out, there's no shame in using a tealight.

## 1: Start with Some Reflection

While holding your intention in your mind, lay the mirror on your table or altar so that it faces up. Then lay your photo face down on top of the mirror so that photo-you is reflected back to its little self.

## 2: Choose Your Glamour

Using the pen and paper, write down exactly what you want the world (or just the recipient of your persuasion) to see when they look at you. Do you want to come across as confident, smart, passionate, and well-spoken? Whatever it is you want, write it like it already is. "I am confident, smart, passionate, and well-spoken." When you're done, place the paper right on top of the photo.

## 3: Dress Up Your Intentions

Still holding onto that intention, anoint the candle by adding some of the oils to your fingers and dragging them along the surface of the wax from the top to the middle and then from the bottom to the middle. Add the candle (in its holder) to the top of the pile, then sprinkle the flower petals, cinnamon, and sugar around it.

## 4: See It in Your Mind's Eye

Light the candle and say (or think) what you wrote down on your paper. While the candle burns, visualize yourself being those things and persuading the hell out of your audience.

## 5: Call in the Big Guns

When you really need a win, you can ask Hecate—goddess of magic—to bless your efforts. (This is best done when you've already formed a relationship with the Triple Goddess because you won't be offering her anything but good intentions here. So buy the lady a drink first.)

## 6: Take the Magic with You

When the candle has finished burning, sweep the petals, cinnamon, and sugar into the red sachet, close it tightly, and tie the strings to seal in the magic. Carry the pouch with you throughout the day, tapping into its energy when you need a little extra persuasive energy.

### MAGICAL MOD

Alternatively, you can skip the glamour and work on clearing your throat, magically speaking. The Throat Chakra is responsible for communication, clarity, and truth—all important shit when you're trying to make a persuasive argument. Set your intention to balance it while you anoint it with the blue chamomile and frankincense oils (mixed with a carrier oil) and breathe deeply into the space. Then just visualize your energy clearing away any blocks.

# MAKE IT RAIN
# MONEY RITUAL

Hey, mimosas and magical activism don't always come cheap. A lot of your efforts are going to require at least a little scratch to get you started. Why not have the Universe help you out?

Whether you need the money to buy plane tickets so you can attend a protest, to contribute to a GoFundMe, or just to fund your weekly meetings, the Universe does. not. care. It's more than happy to foot the bill. So go big! The only limits here are your own.

## MAGICAL MATERIALS

Small knife or carving tool

A green candle

Candle holder

Bergamot essential oil

Cinnamon essential oil

Agate crystal

Garnet crystal

Pen

Paper

Cauldron or fireproof bowl

### CLEVER WITCH TIP
Not wild about knives? Use a magic marker to inscribe small candles (or any candles, really) with your intention. The name says it all.

## 1: Set Yourself Up for Success

You'll need a flat surface or a good chunk of your altar for this one. Work the ritual under a waxing moon to infuse your intention with its expansive energy. If you can't wait that long, any Sunday will do (because it's the beginning of the week).

## 2: Prep the Candle

Holding your intention in your mind, use the knife to carve three dollar signs into the candle. Then anoint the candle by dipping your fingers in the oils and dragging them over the candle from the top to the middle, and then the bottom to the middle, for manifestation.

## 3: See the Good

Place the candle in the center of the space, then place the agate to its left and the garnet to its right. With your intention in mind, light the candle. Take a few minutes to watch the flame, breathe in the oils, and visualize the good you can do with that money.

## 4: Ask for What You Want

Write down why you want the money. You're not justifying the amount to the Universe here. You're accessing the emotion behind the desire, which can infuse the ritual with some powerful fucking magic. When you're done, fold the paper and—continuing to hold that intention in your mind—use the candle to set the corner of it on fire.

## 5: Hand It Off

Drop the paper into your cauldron or bowl to burn completely. Some witches carry the ashes with them in a small jar or pouch until they receive the money, but it's generally better to just hand shit off to the Universe and forget about it. (Think of her like a super fucking efficient personal assistant—one who does not appreciate being micromanaged.)

## 6: Let It Burn

Let the candle burn out entirely before you pack it in to ensure that the magic is potent enough to get you what you need. From that moment on, it's all about trust.

### MAGICAL MOD

This ritual is great for when you need a large amount of money for a specific purpose. But if you're the kind of person who likes to round up their purchase price or donate a little to every cause, you're going to want to bring money your way all the time. Blend the bergamot and cinnamon essential oils with a carrier oil to anoint yourself with now and again, or simply carry a citrine crystal charged with the intention to attract money every day.

# SPELL JARS FOR
# SOCIAL JUSTICE

Making a spell jar is like making one of those recipe jars with all the ingredients for chocolate chip cookies in delicious-looking layers. Spell jars aren't just pretty to look at—they pack some potent and long-lasting magic. They're also really pretty to look at. But they're not fucking tchotchkes, so don't set out to decorate a room with them or anything.

You can use this ritual as a blueprint for any kind of spell-jar creation. Just swap out the intention, colors, stones, and herbs with ones that speak to your needs.

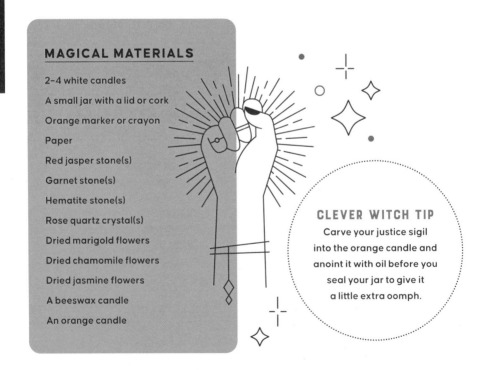

## MAGICAL MATERIALS

2–4 white candles

A small jar with a lid or cork

Orange marker or crayon

Paper

Red jasper stone(s)

Garnet stone(s)

Hematite stone(s)

Rose quartz crystal(s)

Dried marigold flowers

Dried chamomile flowers

Dried jasmine flowers

A beeswax candle

An orange candle

### CLEVER WITCH TIP
Carve your justice sigil into the orange candle and anoint it with oil before you seal your jar to give it a little extra oomph.

## 1: Start with an Intention

Use the orange marker to write your intention or a sigil for justice on a small piece of paper, then stuff that into the jar. (A pen, pencil, or marker of any color will do the trick, but orange is the color of justice.) Remember to hold that intention in your mind throughout the ritual—when you add to the jar, seal it, and cast the spell.

## 2: Top It with Justice-Seeking Stones

Add the stones to the jar one by one, infusing your spell and your intention with their magical properties: red jasper for justice and calm, garnet and hematite for standing in your power, and rose quartz for empathy, forgiveness, and reconciliation.

## 3: Add Some Lovely Florals

Sprinkle in the flowers one species at a time, adding their magic to your intention: marigold for luck, chamomile for justice, and jasmine for love and peace.

## 4: Seal the Jar

Light your beeswax candle and let it get good and melty before letting the wax drip into rubber, cork, or threads of the jar's lid. The goal is to use the wax to "glue" the jar shut. Then use the beeswax candle to melt the bottom of the orange candle, then stick the orange candle on top of the jar. (Yep, like it's a fucking birthday candle.)

## 5: Call for Help

Light the white candles around the jar, one each for the gods, goddesses, or spirits whose help you want, as you call on them for what you need. (Nemesis and Hecate are both badass goddesses who fight for justice. And as the Triple Goddess, Hecate packs an even more powerful punch.)

## 6: Finish with a Spell

Finally, take the deepest breath you've taken all fucking day, light the candle, let yourself feel the fear and anger that called you to this ritual, and then let it all go. Repeat your intention (to yourself is fine) or say a little prayer to bring justice, peace, knowledge, and empathy to those who need it most. Then put out the candle. Repeat the ritual once a day for seven days.

---

### MAGICAL MOD

If social justice seems a little out of reach, you can just make a spell jar to ward off bad vibes. Drop your intention in the jar with salt and pepper, amethyst crystals, chamomile, rosemary, bay, mugwort, and cloves—all shit you can find at the grocery store. Instead of sealing it, just close it. Then give it a shake now and then to reactivate it when you need a little extra protection from toxic bullshit.

---

# LUCKY WITCH
## SIGIL RITUAL

Consider this your very own personal ampoule of Felix Felicis ("liquid luck"), but way fucking easier to make and less likely to spill. Sigils are a simple way to manifest any intention. And because they watch over you without needing your constant fucking attention, they really lend themselves to things like protection and luck.

A lot of planning and hard work goes into magical activism, obviously. But there's something to be said for having Lady Luck on your side. That bitch can move mountains you didn't even know were in your way. This sigil's all about imbuing your efforts with her golden touch so that they have the best possible chance at success. (Create it before you need it, so she doesn't smell your desperation.)

## MAGICAL MATERIALS

A yellow candle (for empowerment)

Lucky crystals like:

  Carnelian

  Citrine

  Clear quartz

  Labradorite

  Alexandrite

Orange pen or marker

A few pieces of paper

Protractor (if you're Type A)

### CLEVER WITCH TIP

Need some luck in a hurry? Make yourself a cup of cinnamon tea, blessing it with your intention before taking a sip.

### 1: Set Your Intention

Get clear on what kind of luck you want. If you want general luck and success, keep your intention general. If you want to succeed at a certain endeavor, get specific. It's your fucking sigil.

### 2: Give It Some Ambience

With your intention in mind, arrange the crystals around the candle and light the candle. (Do you technically need the crystals? No. But they can't hurt and they might help, so why not?)

### 3: Keep It Short and Sweet

Boil your intention down to a short affirmation that epitomizes it. Because it's an affirmation, you're going to phrase it as if it's already a reality. So, "I am successful" or "I am a kickass activist." Write down what you come up with on a piece of scratch paper.

### 4: Break Down Your Intention (Literally)

Cross out all of the vowels, then all of the repeating letters. You should be left with a clusterfuck of unique consonants. Finally, break these letters down into their most basic strokes—so curves, lines, and dots. This, believe it or not, is the basis for your sigil.

### 5: Screw Perfection

Assemble those lines and dots into a one-of-a-kind symbol (overlapping letters are fine). Draw a sigil that speaks to you, even if that means using a protractor, making multiple attempts, and taking some artistic license with the lines to create a shape you like. But also don't spend all fucking day on it. You don't want to infuse your luck sigil with self-doubt and frustration.

### 6: Make It Real

Now that you know what you want it to look like, draw your sigil on a fresh piece of paper while infusing every stroke with the energy of the affirmation it represents. Carry the sigil with you in your wallet or pocket, or put it somewhere in your home and forget about it. Don't think you can just fucking coast now, though. As always, you gotta meet Magic halfway.

**MAGICAL MOD**

Listen, it doesn't have to be art. It just has to be effective. But if your shitty-looking sigil is bothering you, come up with a symbol you like instead. Infuse the symbol with the same energy you set out to instill in the sigil. The point is simply to create something that can exist in your periphery so that you're not focused on it. (Because when we focus on shit we don't have, all we manifest is the not having it.)

# PROTECTION FOR A STEAL

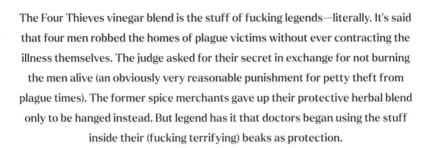

The Four Thieves vinegar blend is the stuff of fucking legends—literally. It's said that four men robbed the homes of plague victims without ever contracting the illness themselves. The judge asked for their secret in exchange for not burning the men alive (an obviously very reasonable punishment for petty theft from plague times). The former spice merchants gave up their protective herbal blend only to be hanged instead. But legend has it that doctors began using the stuff inside their (fucking terrifying) beaks as protection.

By infusing this incredible blend with some added magical protection, it becomes much more than plague-era hand sanitizer. (Although you can totally add it to hand sanitizer, too.) Use it to banish blocks, ward against toxic people, and protect your personal safety during your adventures in activism.

## MAGICAL MATERIALS

Fresh rosemary (healing)

Fresh lavender (calming)

Fresh sage (cleansing)

Fresh thyme (for luck)

Fresh mint (for protection)

Garlic (for banishment)

Apple cider vinegar

Mason jar with plastic lid

### CLEVER WITCH TIP
Pour your strained vinegar into a spray bottle and spritz any person or space that needs protecting. Doorsteps are an obvious choice.

### 1: Mindfully Add the Greenery

Hold your intention in your mind. While you add each herb to your Mason jar, take a moment to breathe in its scent and feel its magic. Tap into that witchy intuition and choose the quantities that feel right to you. (Yes, you can go light on the garlic. But you'll be missing out on some of its antiviral and antibacterial properties.)

### 2: Top Off Your Protection

Carefully pour the vinegar, which offers its own protective properties, over the herbs to fill the jar. Then seal it tightly. (Vinegar can eat away at metal, BTW, so the plastic lid is pretty fucking important.) If you want to go a step further, you can use a magic marker to add a sigil of your own design on the top or the glass.

### 3: Give It a Month

Tuck the jar somewhere safe, cool, and dry where it can hang out for a while. The herbs should infuse the vinegar with your intention and their own magical properties for an entire lunar cycle—a.k.a. a month. But once a day, hold it in your hands, feel its energy, and gently swirl it to stir up the magic and keep that energy flowing.

### 4: Strain Your Infusion

When the month is up, strain the vinegar into its permanent container. You can keep it in its Mason jar to pull from as needed or keep a dropper bottle on you for protection on the go.

### 5: Put That Sh*t on Everything

Put your protective blend to good fucking use! You can anoint yourself if you're going to be in a particularly precarious situation (like talking to politicians) or anoint your tools to add an element of protection to your other spellwork. Hell, you can even marinate some chicken in it, if you want. In addition to its magical properties, it has natural anti-inflammatory, antioxidant, antimicrobial properties that'll do a body good.

> **MAGICAL MOD**
>
> The original recipe for Thieves' Vinegar isn't super practical for modern-day makers, so every recipe you see is going to be an adaptation. Clove, cinnamon, lemon, juniper, and black pepper are all pretty common ingredients in this mix, and some witches stick to only four herbs—one for each thief. Take a minute to research the magical properties of the ingredients and choose the ones that speak to you. (Or that you happen to have in your kitchen cupboards. Either way.)

# MAGICAL ACTIVIST ANOINTING RITUAL

Listen, it's a crazy world out there. You never know what you're going to run into. Maybe it's someone who wants to help you distribute those care packages to the homeless. Maybe it's someone who wants to yell in your face for wearing a BLM tee shirt. This ritual is a quick and easy way to offer your coven the courage to face whatever comes as well as a little magical backup.

An argument could be made for doing this ritual every time you leave the house. But you don't want to dilute the magic with all the other shit you have going on in your daily life. Break this bad girl out when you think your activism could piss some people off and watch their negative bullshit bounce right off you. That said, if you ever feel like you're in danger, get the hell out of Dodge. Magic can't save you from all the crazy.

## MAGICAL MATERIALS

Jojoba oil

Amber bottle with dropper

Cedar essential oil (for courage)

Geranium essential oil (for health)

Rosemary essential oil (for quick thinking)

Small black tourmaline crystal(s) (for protection)

### CLEVER WITCH TIP

When you finish the bottle, leave the tourmaline to infuse a new batch or pluck it out and carry it as a protective talisman.

### 1: Get Clear on Your Intention

Set your intention before you start blending, keeping in mind that this blend can help protect you from yourself as well as others. Toxic energy, physical attacks, dumbass accidents—they're all on the table here.

### 2: Start with the Basics

Add about two tablespoons of sensitive-skin-friendly jojoba oil or another favorite carrier oil to your amber dropper bottle. (The dark bottle keeps out harmful UV light, which can affect your oils, so that you can keep your oil blend around for future battles—er, good deeds.)

### 3: Show Some Respect for the Oils

Each essential oil listed offers protection in addition to some activist-friendly properties. Add two drops of each, repeating your intention or making note of those magical properties with each drop. You want to do this really mindfully and not like you're whipping up a protein shake. (But you can totally infuse a protein shake with protective energy, btw.)

### 4: Add a Little Something Extra

Drop in the black tourmaline—which has some serious protective properties all its own—repeating your intention one more time. It will infuse the oils with its energy as much as they'll infuse it with theirs.

### 5: Charge the Bottle

Twist the dropper top onto the bottle and gently swirl it around to blend the oils—counterclockwise to keep bad energy at bay. Then hold the bottle between your hands and see the glow of badass protective energy wrapping itself tightly around it. Say your intention again, just for good fucking measure.

### 6: Anoint Everyone

Holding your intention in your mind, anoint your wrists and neck with the oil and see its energy coursing through your veins and lighting up your chakras like a winning slot machine. Anoint the others, saying a little prayer for their courage and protection and walking them through the visualization. Then go out there and do some fucking good!

> **MAGICAL MOD**
>
> Switch things up and anoint a larger black tourmaline crystal with your tincture, then carry the stone with you anytime you feel you need a little extra protection. (Don't take the bottle—goddess forbid it breaks in your fucking pocket and cuts you.) You can also use the oil on any magical tools, like candles or talismans, to imbue them with a boost of badass-activist energy.

# ROADBLOCK-BANISHING

## RITUAL

Whether you're just dipping your toes into magical activism, or you've got tons of experience using your skills to effect change, you're bound to run into some red tape along your journey. Maybe it's not the politics. Maybe you just feel like you're chasing your fucking tail lately. Either way, this is the ritual for you.

Road-opening rituals like this one are common in hoodoo practices and feature a tropical herb called *Abre Camino* (Open Road). And they can do a lot more than make sure you don't trip over that red tape. Road openers can clear a path to success, abundance, good health, and a healthy fucking bank account.
(A girl's gotta eat if she's going to change the world.)

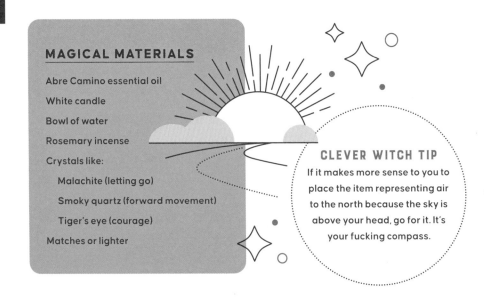

### MAGICAL MATERIALS

Abre Camino essential oil

White candle

Bowl of water

Rosemary incense

Crystals like:

    Malachite (letting go)

    Smoky quartz (forward movement)

    Tiger's eye (courage)

Matches or lighter

### CLEVER WITCH TIP
If it makes more sense to you to place the item representing air to the north because the sky is above your head, go for it. It's your fucking compass.

## 1: Start with the Open Road

This is one of those rituals that invokes the four elements, so you'll need to clear a space to put everything in a small compass-like circle. Before you start placing items at its points, anoint the candle with the oil. You'll be banishing blocks in order to clear your path (rather than manifesting, or bringing toward you, whatever's at the end of that path), so dip your fingers in the oil and gently drag them along the wax from the middle to the top and then from the middle to the bottom.

## 2: Invoke the Elements

Holding your intention in your mind, light the incense and place it to the east to represent air. Then feel the energy of the intention move to your hands as you hold and charge the crystal before placing it to the north to represent earth. If you want to use multiple crystals, you can make a little pile to the north, or you can place one in your compass and hold another to set your intention—whatever the hell works for you.

## 3: Invoke the Elements (Part 2)

Still holding that intention, light the anointed candle and place it to the south to represent fire. Finally, dip your fingers into the water and feel its flowing energy before placing it to the west. The water does double-duty as a mirror that can open the door to new beginnings.

## 4: Visualize Your Path

Close your eyes and say your intention (or a spell of your own design) out loud. Then see in your mind's eye a clear path. See yourself walking down that path unobstructed. See yourself doing the fucking Electric Slide down that path if it helps you feel the free, joyful, flowing energy of this ritual.

## 5: Finish Strong

Once you feel your path has cleared, talk with your girls about what's at the other end of it while the candle (safely) burns out. Then discard the remnants and thank the elements for their help before closing the ritual. Continue to keep your crystals nearby, with all their block-busting energy.

### MAGICAL MOD

You can find Abre Camino in all sorts of products, but the essential oil can be handy for clearing paths even when you don't have time for a full ritual. Anoint yourself with it by dabbing some anywhere you'd put perfume. Then go about your day with the confidence that you can effortlessly handle any bump in the road.

# BADASS BANISHING ⚡ (NOT BINDING) RITUAL ⚡

During a certain twice-impeached president's term, witches came together in spirit from all over the world to perform binding spells in the hopes of stopping him from doing harm. They had the best intentions, but good witches (witches for *good*) don't fuck with binding spells. Those things are steeped in resentment and manipulation. Say it with me, witches: We. Do. Not. Hex. People.

Plus, those things don't just bind the recipient. They bind their harmful bullshit to you. Keep your fucking hands clean and banish that negative energy instead. Banishing has the added bonus of working on anything. Sure, you can banish a person and their toxic crap, but you can also banish feelings of overwhelm when planning a protest or an annoying Karen situation. This isn't just a ritual. It's a life hack.

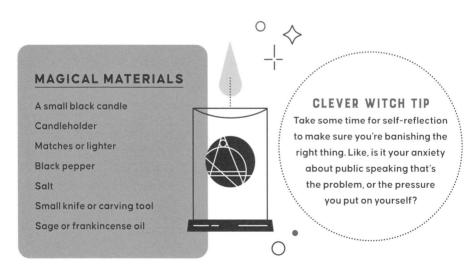

## MAGICAL MATERIALS

A small black candle

Candleholder

Matches or lighter

Black pepper

Salt

Small knife or carving tool

Sage or frankincense oil

### CLEVER WITCH TIP
Take some time for self-reflection to make sure you're banishing the right thing. Like, is it your anxiety about public speaking that's the problem, or the pressure you put on yourself?

## 1: Start with the Salt

Sprinkle the salt around you in a counterclockwise circle, infusing it with protective energy so that it forms a barrier. (Get yourself one of those big containers for this so you don't use up the table salt.)

## 2: See the Problem Clearly

Whether you're banishing a toxic politician's influence or your own nervous butterflies, see the problem clearly in your mind. Boil it down to an intention, like, "Congresswoman Smith will resign" or "My anxiety will disappear."

## 3: Make Your F*cking Mark

Once you're clear on your intention, make it count by carving it right into the wax. If it's a lot, break it down into a sigil and carve that instead.

## 4: Dress Your Candle

Sage and frankincense are awesome for clearing out negative shit, but you can use cooking oil if it's all you've got. Dip your fingers in the oil and drag them along the length of the candle while holding your intention in your mind. Because this is a banishing spell, you're going to go from the middle to the top, then the middle to the bottom, until the candle is covered in oil. Then sprinkle the pepper over it.

## 5: Burn It Down

Place your candle in the holder in an area where it can safely burn for several hours. Then light the wick while saying your intention out loud. Let the candle burn completely. (This should be common sense, but never leave a burning candle unattended. This is why you use a small one. Nobody has six hours to waste staring at a fucking candle.)

## 6: Re-Energize the Void

Once that toxic shit is gone, it leaves a void. Either you fill it, or something else does. Better that it's you. Spend a few minutes visualizing the energy you want to fill that void. You can even play music, move your ass, or do yoga if you're feeling it. Just make sure you raise that vibe!

### MAGICAL MOD

This ritual is just one of many ways to banish the bad. When trying to stop a crappy person from doing crappy things, you can "blow" them away from their harmful goal by blowing out the candle's flame. Or skip the candle: visualize yourself plucking out the bad energy wherever you see it and throwing it away (or setting it on fire—whatever works for you). In other words, tailor this shit to your needs.

RITUAL

# RITUALS FOR
## EVERY DAY

···················· • ····················

No matter what you do with your magic, you're
going to want to do two things on the regular:
ask for help from a higher power and show some
fucking gratitude when you get it (so you keep
getting it). This section gives you easy ways to do
both, plus a blueprint for designing your own rituals
whenever you need a little something special.

# SPIRITUAL BACKUP SUMMONING RITUAL

One of the many awesome things about being part of a coven is knowing that you're not alone. But the reality is, you never were. You're surrounded by spirits who are ready and willing to back you up, from land spirits to ancient goddesses, and from ancestors to the badass witches who came before you.

All you have to do is ask. And maybe offer up something sweet to the more stubborn, old-school spirits. This ritual helps you do just that, but you can always use it just to chat with dead loved ones and check in with spiritual leaders.

**RITUAL**

## MAGICAL MATERIALS

Cup

Pitcher of fresh water

A white candle

Personalized offerings

### CLEVER WITCH TIP
Let your activism and allyship be your offering to spirits who benefit from your intentions, saying, "I'm here to help, but I can't do it alone."

## 1: Choose Your Offering

You can't get something for nothing. The water acts as an offering. For big asks, long-term relationships, and demanding spirits, you'll want to choose something more personal.

## 2: Pour One Out

Hold them in your mind while you pour, scoop, spread, or otherwise prepare the offering. Then take it in both hands, hold it out toward the altar, and say the spirit's name. (Something like, "To all those powerful women who came before us" works when you're calling on a bunch of badasses at once.)

## 3: Tap into That Magic

Imagine your energy as a warm white or golden light flowing from you and into the offering—from your mind and heart, down through your arms, and out from your fingers. (If you're doing this with your coven, one person can hold the offering while each member sends their own light flowing to the cup.) Then place the cup on the altar.

## 4: Express Your Gratitude

Light the candle and stand in gratitude. Whether you say a simple "Thank you" or you list the ways you're grateful, let the spirit know you appreciate them.

## 5: Tell 'Em What You Want

Once you've dispensed with the flattery, let the spirits know why you're there. Be respectful but clear when asking them to stand with you and/or watch over you while you do your best to live up to their example. Then ask them for a sign that your offering has been accepted and blow out the candle.

## 6: Pay F*cking Attention

When you ask for a sign, you need to look for a sign—even if you get an answer you don't like. In that case, go to Plan B. (Always have a Plan B.)

## 7: Do It Again

Repeat this ritual as often as you like. Holidays celebrating ancestors (Dia de los Muertos, Samhain, etc.) and the spirits' birthdays are good days to put a little extra effort into it with sweets, flowers, or booze.

### MAGICAL MOD

Once you've formed a relationship with a helpful spirit, create a talisman to keep them near. Choose an object that has meaning to you, like a pendant or crystal. Every day for a week, spend a few minutes visualizing their energy infusing the talisman. Seal the talisman (with words, water, or moonlight), and then bring it along on your activist adventures. Just remember to recharge it once in a while.

# SHOW SOME F*CKING
## ◇◇ GRATITUDE RITUAL ◇◇

Some spirits and goddesses are low-key and don't require much in
the way of gratitude beyond a simple "Thanks." And some are
the Mariah Careys of the magical world. If you don't know
which variety you're dealing with, more is more.

How can you tell? Well, how have your spells been working lately?
If they've been going to shit, it couldn't hurt to show a little
love to the entities that can bring your magic to life.

## MAGICAL MATERIALS

Pen

Paper

Two white candles

A pink candle

A blue candle

Frankincense essential oil

Frankincense or myrrh incense

Crystals like:

  Clear quartz

  Amethyst

  Iolite

Cauldron or fireproof bowl

Matches or lighter

### CLEVER WITCH TIP
You want to do this spell when
the moon is full or at least getting
there to represent the fullness of
your heart in gratitude.

*thank you*

### 1: Feel F*cking Grateful

Start by filling yourself up with gratitude—for magic, for a benevolent Universe, for the Goddess or goddesses, and for anything else you can think of that's bringing you joy right now. This is your intention.

### 2: Write a Thank You Note

Write down what you're thankful for. It doesn't have to be poetry, but remember that you're writing to a goddess or some other entity who could crush you like a bug. Be respectful. And bring the joy. This can't be like writing a note to the aunt who made you a quilt from your baby clothes for high school graduation. You have to put some positive fucking energy into it. Carry that with you throughout the rest of the ritual.

### 3: Set the Scene

Set your cauldron in front of you and slip the note into it (fold it if you need to). Place your stones around the cauldron, then anoint your candles. Because you're neither banishing nor manifesting anything, you're going to rub the oil along the wax from the wick all the way down to the bottom. The white candles will go to the north and south of the cauldron, the blue to the west, and the pink to the east. The incense can go wherever the hell you want it to.

### 4: Actually Give Thanks

Light the candles and the incense, close your eyes, and take a moment to breathe in the scent of frankincense (or myrrh). Center yourself. Then express your gratitude to the Goddess (or whoever) and ask, respectfully, for continued blessings. (You don't want to rehash your note. You just want to say a quick word of appreciation.)

### 5: Send It Up

Use a match or one of the white candles to carefully light the note on fire in the cauldron. See its energy being released and finding its intended recipient. Once it and the candles have finished burning, you can move on with your day. Just keep an eye out for signs that the Goddess heard and accepted your thanks.

> ### MAGICAL MOD
> You don't have to wait until you want something to pour one out for the magical beings whose help you want (and need). In fact, you shouldn't. Make offerings a regular habit, especially to those spirits you call on often. There are worse things than having a drink with a fucking goddess once a week. But if you don't want to waste your good tequila, flowers, candy, or even fruit will do.

RITUAL

# DIY YOUR OWN
# DAMN RITUAL

You've probably noticed by now that these rituals leave a lot of wiggle room. Once you know your shit about crystals, candles, incense, and other magical objects, you can tailor most of them to your intentions by swapping in the magical amplifiers that make sense to you. That's by design. (Fucking brilliant, right?)

But what if nothing feels quite right and you want to start from scratch? Or if you need to work a spell on the fly? No problem! The magic? That energetic force? It flows through you. You can direct it toward whatever the hell you want. You can write the spell, design the structure, choose the components—all of it is in your hands. You just have to ask yourself a few questions.

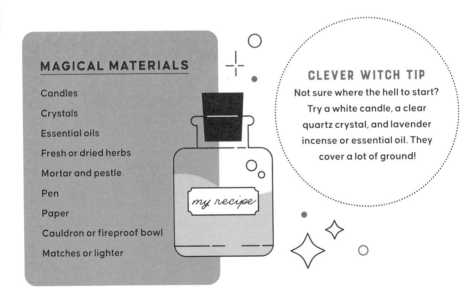

## MAGICAL MATERIALS

Candles

Crystals

Essential oils

Fresh or dried herbs

Mortar and pestle

Pen

Paper

Cauldron or fireproof bowl

Matches or lighter

### CLEVER WITCH TIP
Not sure where the hell to start? Try a white candle, a clear quartz crystal, and lavender incense or essential oil. They cover a lot of ground!

*my recipe*

## 1: What's Your Intention?

What do you want the ritual to accomplish? Do you want to manifest change? Bust energetic blocks? Boost your communication skills? Get really fucking clear on why you're working the spell, or the spell won't work.

## 2: Should You Mark Your Calendar?

Will this ritual benefit from a lunar boost? What kind—coming, going, dark, or full? Would the new-beginning energy of Sunday be better than Wednesday's centered energy? Does it even fucking matter? The timing should feel right to you.

## 3: What Materials Do You Need?

What crystals could best amplify your intentions? What scents? Will a colored candle help, or might a white one do the trick? What materials do you need? A candle's not much good without a match. Make a list of materials ahead of time so you don't discover a missing piece halfway through the damn ritual.

## 4: Are Rhymes Involved?

Do you want to say a few words? Or write a few words? Do you want those words to feel modern and badass? Or age-old and mystical? It can be helpful to sort out the wording before you start your spell.

## 5: Which Framework Works?

Are you going to send your message up in flames? Meditate on your intention? Say the spell you just wrote over a gorgeous crystal grid? What method or ritual would best serve your purpose? What feels like the most authentic way to celebrate your intention? The one thing all rituals have is a structure, even if it's a loose one. Sort out yours, and you're ready to make some fucking magic.

## 6: Does It Make the Grimoire?

Writing all of this down isn't just helpful for when you're ready to work the ritual. (Although that is really fucking helpful.) It's also helpful to have it ready to add to your written repertoire. Not only will you be able to work the spell again, you'll also be able to make adjustments as you do. Who knows which of your kickass spells will change the world?

### MAGICAL MOD

Need to work a spell on the go? Anything you have on hand can become a magical amplifier. You can also use items that mean something specific to you. If the seashell you picked up in Key West as a kid feels like safety and calm to you, charge that fucker up as a protective talisman. Hell, you can turn a piece of mulch into a quartz crystal if you channel that energy into it.

# PART FOUR

# DO SOME DAMN GOOD

# "You had the power all along, my dear."

— ‹ • › —

GLINDA, *WIZARD OF OZ*

# CHAPTER 11

# LOOK IN A MAGIC MIRROR

hanging the world starts with you, which means you better have your own damn house in order. That starts with taking a good, hard look at yourself. Do you benefit from privilege? Might you have any unconscious biases? Are you holding onto some unhelpful shit? If you answered No to any of those questions, try again. The answer is Yes, to all of them, for all of us. And that's OK. We all have blind spots. The important thing is to identify what you need to work on and how you can use it to the advantage of others. Once you understand your limitations, you can do something about them. And then you can *really* start to make a difference.

## Start with You (Again), Boo

You went deep to figure out what you needed in a coven. Now you need to go even deeper, because what you're about to do isn't about you. If you're going to help people, you have to clear out all the crap that could get in your way. No one expects you to be perfect—least of all, Magic. But you have to know what you're starting with. Be really honest with yourself and learn to recognize when you feel resistance to something. That's how you know you're not being honest enough. That kind of energetic block is like a knot in your back. Sometimes you need the elbow. It's not always pleasant, but it's fucking effective, and you always feel better afterward.

## ✧ Check Your Privilege

Privilege is having an advantage over others because of your race, gender, religion, sexual orientation, socioeconomic position, health, education, and/or physical ability. It means you had a head start, making it easier to get where you were going. Put another way: You didn't always *make* good choices, sometimes you *had* good choices. We've all benefited from certain advantages, whether or not we've had it hard in other ways. Those who are unaware of, or unwilling to examine, their privilege only help perpetuate it. By working to understand your privilege, you can use it not only to speak up for others but also to help dismantle systems that leave others behind.

## ✧ Investigate Your Bias

Implicit bias is unconscious—it affects your actions and understanding without you even knowing it. And it's one hell of an energy-fuck when you're trying to change the world. If you're a human on this planet, you can't fucking help it. The sooner you accept that, the sooner you can start making the world a better place to live for *everyone*. So keep an eye out for preconceived notions that need challenging. (And if you have any obvious bias, you should obviously work on that, too.)

## ✧ Heal Your Own Hurt

Hurt people hurt people, often unintentionally. If you're harboring any resentments, now's the time to clean your shit up. Make sure your actions are in alignment with who you want to be, not who you've been taught to be. Therapy is a top choice. Talking things out with your sisters is another. And a lot of the practices you pick up while growing your magic can help, too. Meditate, journal, express gratitude—whatever you need to do to work through your bad energy and avoid foisting it onto others. After all, a glass house will definitely break if you start throwing stones while you're still trapped inside the damn thing.

## CRYSTAL F'CKING CLEAR

When self-discovery is the goal, lapis lazuli is the crystal for you. It's called the "stone of truth" for a fucking reason. Hold it while you close your eyes and set an intention to get clarity, then go into meditation mode, clear your mind, and wait for answers. It can be pretty handy when used with a pendulum to uncover unconscious issues, too. Get specific with the questions you ask, trying to home in on exactly where your privilege and biases lie.

## Get Your Head in the Game

Your thoughts and feelings are imbued with your magic—they're constantly creating the world you live in. Watch how you talk to yourself. You could look up one day and find yourself surrounded by your negative inner monologue. There's no need to be super optimistic and pretend shit's great all the time. But magic is about asking for what you want and believing you're going to get it. If your magic is on point and you think your week's going to suck, then your week's going to suck.

## Bring Your F*cking A-Game

It's admirable for witches to want to use their magic to change the world. But the world needs your A-game. Make sure you've got this shit down. Practice empowering spells on yourself before you try a banishing spell on a bad president. Be honest with yourself about the shit you need to work on. And commit to getting better all the time. Not only will you up your game, you'll also raise your own vibe in the process and make your magic that much more powerful and effective.

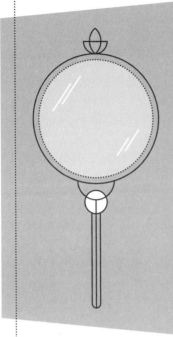

## PRACTICAL MAGIC

Whenever you're having trouble believing in yourself or committing to something, look in the mirror and tell yourself what you need to hear. Literally. You already know your words are magic. But you can instill your magic with even more powerful energy when you look yourself in the eyes. Imagine a circuit of energy that flows up from your toes, out of your head, and back around into your toes, getting stronger with every turn. That's what's happening when you say uplifting shit to yourself. So do it more often.

### ✦ Acknowledge Your Limitations

Knowing your limitations is one thing. Acknowledging your limitations is a whole other fucking ballgame. You have to know the difference between the stuff you completely suck at and the stuff you can get better at. An argument could be made for trying to get better at everything. But it makes a hell of a lot more sense to focus your energy where it'll do the most good. And that goes double for when you have a coven full of talented witches who can back you up. Acknowledge your limitations, know your strengths, and play to both.

### ✦ Make a Damn Commitment

It's not always easy (especially for Geminis), but you need to make a commitment to your coven, to your cause(s), and to learning. You have to go into this magic thing with some perspective. Magic is eternal and infinite. Human beings:

not so much. That's a pretty good indication that you don't know everything, even about yourself. Being open to lifelong learning and improvement is the only way you can grow, get better, and do better. And the world needs you at your best.

### ✧ Give It Your F*cking All

Once you've got your head on straight and you're ready do some good, put your fucking back into it. Read all the books, listen to all the podcasts, talk to all the people. Get fully immersed in the issues and decide where your newly whole, self-aware ass can do the most good. Even better, ask the people most affected how you can help and actively listen to what they say. Then get out there and change the fucking world.

## WITCH, YOU GOT THIS!

If you're going to help other people, you need to work through all your own blocks and negative energy first. It's more than just cleaning up your side of the street. It's making sure you don't accidentally do more harm than good.

Use your privilege for your purpose
Watch for unconscious bias
Deal with your damn issues
Believe in the good
Work on your magic first
Play to your strengths
Make it a habit to do better

By doing the work on yourself first, you ensure that you're working from the highest possible vibration. And that makes for some of the most powerful world-changing magic.

# THE CRYSTAL GRID
## ◇◇ OF TRUTH ◇◇

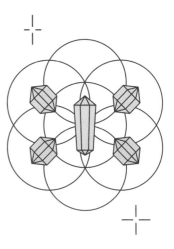

This isn't nearly as scary as it sounds. Crystal grids help you focus your energy on an intention (like self-discovery) while harnessing the collective power of multiple crystals. The Crystal Grid of Truth is filled with stones that target the Throat Chakra to help you express your true self.

Are you afraid to speak your truth? Unsure of what might be lurking in your subconscious? Like Veritaserum with pretty crystals, this grid will get it out of you so you can deal with it and move on. Break this bad boy out whenever you're trying to decide on your next world-changing move to ensure your path forward is clear.

## MAGICAL MATERIALS

Aquamarine crystals (for courage)

Angelite crystals (for awareness)

Blue lace agate crystals (for articulation)

Blue kyanite crystals (for good vibes)

Rose quartz crystals (for self-compassion)

Malachite crystals (for self-acceptance)

A lapis lazuli crystal (for truth)

### CLEVER WITCH TIP

A simpler alternative to this truth-telling ritual involves holding a lapis lazuli in one hand and free-writing with the other until you get to the bottom of shit.

### 1: Choose Your Crystals

No one is saying that you have to buy dozens of crystals. But if you want to go all out, buy a carved-wood grid online, and feature it as a piece of magical art, you can do that. You'll find plenty of inspo online. You can also just use the crystals you have and call it a fucking day. As long as you infuse your grid with intention, it'll do the job.

### 2: Set Your Intention

Clasp the lapis lazuli—the boss of self-discovery stones—between your palms, close your eyes, and set the intention to deepen your awareness, clear away any blocks, see the truth (ugly or otherwise), and communicate it consciously and courageously.

### 3: Create Your Grid

Place the lapis lazuli in the center of your space. If you've got the stones, place them in a pretty, multilayered pattern around the lapis lazuli. If you've just got one of each, a single circle will do. (Yes, grid implies square. But you want to choose the best shape for the job. For expanding your mind, that's a circle.) These stones modify and enhance the intention of the central stone.

### 4: Activate the Damn Thing

You settled on your intention while holding the center stone. Now say it out loud over your grid while imagining a white light of energy connecting the stones in a spiral, from the center outward.

### 5: Keep a Third Eye Out

Whenever you pass your grid, take a moment to see it activated in your mind's eye and know that it's bringing the truth to the surface. Hold a question in your head (something like, "help me acknowledge my implicit bias") and see what bubbles up. Then, Pay. Fucking. Attention.

---

**MAGICAL MOD**

If you turn into Sméagol every time you see a pretty crystal, maybe avoid walking into a store full of them. Buy only as many as your budget (*budget*, not your credit-card limit) allows. Magic is about intention, so you can always sub in what you have on hand. In some cases, personal objects enhance the spell. In this case, anything blue or that holds the meaning of truth and awareness will do.

"Magic lies in challenging what seems impossible."

—— ( • ) ——

CAROL MOSELY BRAUN

# CHAPTER 12

# DON'T COMPLICATE UNCOMPLICATED SH*T

**A**s a human being, it's in your nature to make shit as unnecessarily complicated as possible. It's like we assume that something's too good to be true if it doesn't take a fuck-ton of work or sacrifice. But complicated spells don't work better than simple ones. Take that as a lesson before you throw your whole self into saving the world on Day One. Start small, take baby steps, learn as you go. And remember that you're human and you're going to fuck up a few times along the way. Luckily, Magic is forgiving.

## Break Shit Down

Breaking down the patriarchy and other bullshit systems requires breaking down the issues themselves. How do you climb a mountain? You take it one step at a time. If you try to do more than that, then the whole thing feels insurmountable, and you go back to eating cheese puffs on the couch. But as you're taking those small steps, you also have to have faith that you'll get to the top to enjoy that view eventually. It takes patience, persistence, endurance, intention, and the ability to see the bigger picture.

### ✦ Start Small

The more complex the issue, the more you gotta throw at it. But that doesn't mean you throw it all at once. More often than not, it's just physically fucking impossible. Breaking it down into small, actionable steps allows you to tailor the magic to each one of those steps. Not only will that have a snowball effect, it will also allow you to chip away at the foundation of the issue. That means that, rather than wasting your energy trying to attack this giant thing, you can bring it crashing down with less effort overall.

### ✦ Sketch Sh*t Out

Spend some time during your meetings planning those small steps and how your magic can fuel your efforts. It can help to work backward from your goal. Let's say you decide you want to hold a march. That means you have to organize that march. What's the first step you take? Maybe you pick a day during the full moon to use its powerful manifestation energy. Next step: permits. How can you help that process go smoothly? Make a plan for each step, and only as far in advance as you can clearly see. You might be able to tackle more by assigning each witch a step, but don't let your ambition get in the way of your action.

## PRACTICAL MAGIC

If you're having trouble seeing a clear path to your goal, you can try using a few different magical tools. For big picture shit, break out the tarot cards. With your desired result and the question of where to start in mind, pull one card or a whole spread. If you have some steps in mind but you're not sure which one's the right one, tap into your intuition using a pendulum. You can ask Yes/No questions or you can use it to scry over a map. When all else fails, keep shit simple and meditate on the question.

# Be F*cking Reasonable

You can't demand the world of your coven and expect to get anywhere. Making an impact takes time and commitment, but people have other shit going on in their lives. You have to make space for that, too. And as magical and amazing as you all are, you're still human. (You've read that a few times now, but it's important. Badass magical activists need to retain a little humility so they don't shine brightly and burn out quickly.) Magic is limitless. You are not. You need to set reasonable goals, listen to your girls when they're wearing out, and make self-care a priority.

# Have a Witchy Gift Exchange

No, not actual presents. (Well, maybe actual presents. That could be fun.) You don't need to waste money, time, and anxiety on courses and conventions that don't end up teaching you all that much. By focusing first on what you can learn from each other, you can home in on what you *need* to learn elsewhere. Utilize each other's strengths, but also support each other and strengthen each other's weaknesses. If you choose your fellow witches wisely, you will be fucking amazed at your coven's cumulative knowledge and experience.

### ✦ Play to Your Strengths

You're not a lone wolf anymore. You've surrounded yourself with people you can rely on, people whose skills complement your own. Use that to your fucking advantage! If you suck at writing letters, then you should definitely not be in charge of the letter-writing campaign. But one of your sisters was an English Lit major whose words drip with natural magic, so she's got you. You're a people person, so go knock on some doors. Basically, don't force anyone to do anything they don't like or aren't good at if you can avoid it. It drains your energy and saps your magic.

### ✦ Learn from Each Other

Playing to your strengths works just as well inside the coven as out. Every one of your sisters has something to teach you. In fact, they probably have a lot to teach

## CRYSTAL F*CKING CLEAR

As always, there are a couple of handy crystals that can help you on your journey to learn, to grow, and to change the world one step at a time. Fluorite is awesome for learning, improving focus and memory, clearing mental blocks, and discovering your purpose. Apophyllite works beautifully for personal development, introspection, intuition, and good choices. Incorporate them into your spellwork, meditate with them in hand, or even infuse some moon water with their magic and drink it while you work out your plan of action with your sisters.

you. Some of that you'll discover over time. But it doesn't hurt to go around the circle and ask each member for one badass skill they've mastered and feel comfortable taking the lead on. Yoga, song, meditation, tarot, crystals, navigating the American justice system—everyone's good at something. By sharing those things, you'll save a shit-ton of money and allow each of your sisters to shine.

### ✦ See Your Weaknesses

There's no shame in having weaknesses. There is shame, however, in burying your fucking head in the sand and refusing to own those weaknesses and to improve on them. That's what you're here to do. And it's a hell of a lot harder to help people when you're tripping over your own ego. So be real about what you don't know and take a lesson from the Owens sisters about the consequences of half-assing magic. If you don't know something, find someone who can teach you (kind of like you did when you bought this book). Don't think that you have to keep *everything* in the family. Keep doing your research and learning from witches outside the coven, too.

## Bet on You

When all's said and done, you just have to remember that the magic is in you and everything else will fall into place. Putting yourself into a spell will always amplify it. Let the spellwork be easy so that you don't accidentally infuse it with frustration instead of confidence. Work on honing your intuition, then listen to it when it talks to you (or yells at you). Keep things simple—your motivations, your intentions, and your actions. The purer all that shit is, the more powerful your magic will be. Living in this crazy world is hard enough. Trust yourself.

## WITCH, YOU GOT THIS!

Changing the world is no small feat, but it is made up of small feats. There may be dozens of them. There may be millions. But each step gets you closer to your goal. And with Magic on your side, you may just get there faster.

Take small, easy steps
Infuse each step with magic
Let your efforts snowball
Have some fucking humility
Let each sister take the lead
Steer into your strengths
Trust your magic

This is a marathon, not a sprint. Pace yourself, hydrate (with what is up to you), rely on your team, and keep your eye on the fucking prize. That's how you make sure you get to the finish line.

"You really can change the world if you care enough."

— • —

MARIAN WRIGHT EDELMAN

# CHAPTER 13

# CHOOSE YOUR CAUSE WISELY

**R**emember when, in *Indiana Jones and the Last Crusade*, that douchey guy chose the wrong chalice and just fucking disintegrated? Don't be that guy. Take time to weigh your options and make a measured decision. If you jump into a battle unprepared, not only will you look like an asshole, but also you could do more harm than good. You can only contribute to a cause when you understand the issues, learn how to be a real ally, and tailor your actions to the information.

## Listen, *Then Speak*

Remember those big, hairy, 21st-century problems we talked about? Whatever they are, they're not simple. In most instances, they're intersectional. That means you can't just rush into shit. You have to understand what you're getting involved in, especially if you're acting as an ally. Both magically and ethically, you have to come from a place of compassion. Learn everything you can about an issue first and listen to those who are experiencing it. Even if the issue affects you, too, understanding the perspectives of others is an important step in creating the change you need.

## ✦ Be an Ally

You absolutely can and should fight for causes that primarily affect others—especially if you're passionate about them—but you'll need to check your ego. Being an ally is about more than being sympathetic to a cause, and it's about more than joining a protest here or there. First and foremost, being an ally means understanding that not everything is about you. In fact, nothing at all is about you. Do not insert yourself and your agenda into the middle of someone else's fight.

Learn as much as you can about the issue, then listen to those affected and ask how you can help. Don't ask them to explain anything to you, though—research that shit on your own time. It might be uncomfortable at times, but discomfort is a sign of growth. And it's a pretty safe bet your discomfort is nothing compared to theirs. Dedicate some spellwork to sending love, light, and healing to those most affected by the fight.

## ✦ Understand Intersectionality

An understanding of intersectionality is crucial to activism, magical or not. People are not one thing, and unfortunately, they can be—and often are—discriminated against for all the things they are. For example, in comparison to white men, Black women earn the lowest wages—less than both white women and Black men. The discrimination Black women suffer is exponential based on their overlapping identities. That's as unacceptable as it is unfair, and yet it's even more difficult to combat.

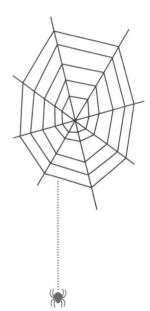

You can't just address one issue. Each issue is connected to many others in a giant, sticky, spider web of injustice. And not everyone feels represented by the fight. Each intersectional identity has its own unique set of needs and disadvantages, which means we need to realize that every person will have a different and valid perspective on the issues that affect them. Keep your magic simple but be careful not to oversimplify the issues you're up against.

## CRYSTAL F'CKING CLEAR

Considering the history of how witches have been treated, we can certainly empathize with those suffering injustice and discrimination. But if you, yourself, have not experienced it in this lifetime, make sure that you're being an ally and not a pain in the ass. One way you can help is by coming from a place of love and positivity. You can't let yourself get mired in all the shit. And there's a lot of it. You have to float along the surface, ready to grab hands and pull others out. Rose quartz can help with that. Use it in both your meditation and your spellwork surrounding issues of injustice.

## Focus on the Right Fight

With so many incredibly complex issues to deal with, it can be hard to know where to start. But by choosing a single, well-defined step that you can take in an area you're passionate about, you both concentrate and strengthen your energy. Your passion has a magic all its own. Try to choose an area of the fight where you can do the most good, and don't let your focus wander to other steps or bigger battles. Scattered energy does no one any good. If your sisters are equally passionate about that cause, you can divide and conquer by each taking a small step to focus on. Or you can cross your streams and focus on the same step in order to amplify your magic.

### ✦ A Little Inspo

You know there's injustice in the world. You know there are people who need your help. The sheer number can be overwhelming. For as many huge, systemic issues that exist, you're going to come across hundreds of smaller battles. And that's not even taking into account the intersectionality of these issues. But consider this your jumping-off point. Here are just a few of the monumental issues facing us all today. When you don't know where the fuck to start, pick something off this list and think of one ridiculously tiny thing you can do to be of use to your fellow humans and animals.

- **Access to clean water**
- **Animal welfare**
- **Climate crisis**
- **Employee safety**
- **Food insecurity**
- **Gun violence**
- **Housing discrimination**
- **Immigration policy**
- **Income inequality**
- **Indigenous rights and safety**
- **LGBTQ+ rights and safety**
- **Mental health**
- **Police brutality and reform**
- **Racism**
- **Sexism**
- **Student loans and education costs**
- **Uncontrolled healthcare costs**
- **Voting rights**
- **Women's rights and safety**

This is obviously far from a comprehensive list, and there are certainly more pressing issues to be found. The damn thing could go on for pages. That realization alone should spark within you a desire to get to fucking work.

## KNOW YOUR SH'T ABOUT WITCH HUNTS

People who were arrested and executed for being witches were often just elderly or disabled women, those who didn't fit in with puritanical notions of a healthy society. They weren't just hanged, either. They were often subjected to torture and sexual assault. After the Salem witch trials, the colony admitted that they fucked up and compensated the families of the accused, but the damage was done. Ignorance and injustice leave lasting marks. Not only was it a dark period in history, but it also continues to feed into a negative perception of witchcraft.

### ✧ Feel Your Feelings

Make a list of the causes that you're interested in tackling. Go down that list and pause a moment on each cause. Note how you feel, what the idea of the cause does to your energy. Notice if you're feeling any blocks or anger. The right cause will be one where your faith that you can make a difference surpasses your anger. If you can't get past the damn anger, you have to do more work on you and come back to that cause with a level head. Negative emotions aren't going to fuel your magic, they're just going to fuck with it.

### ✦ Use That Witchy Intuition

Once you've gone over the list, meditate on it. Visualize the world you want to live in. Feel what's most important to you. See the list sorting itself in your mind like something lovely out of *Harry Potter*, with the best causes for you floating to the top and the others sinking below them. If you're still stuck, ask your favorite spirit or deity for a little inspiration. You may have to wait for an answer—it's not like Magic and goddesses work on our schedule. Just let go of the question and trust that the right answer will come.

## WITCH, YOU GOT THIS!

In a world so unbelievably teeming with life-threatening problems and injustice, it can be hard to know where the hell to start.

Listen to those most affected
Check your fucking ego
Factor in intersectionality
Choose a cause that speaks to you
Meditate on where you can do the most good
Give anger the boot
Take one tiny step

Yeah, it's a lot. But you already knew that.
That's why you're holding this fucking book.
So start anywhere, just as long as you start.

"I can choose to be afraid of my powers, or I can use them."

SABRINA, *CHAOS*

# CHAPTER 14

# SUIT UP, WITCHES

**W**hat does any magical superhero do before heading into battle? They suit up. And they look damn good doing it. You've got to be armed not just with magic but also with the right mindset. No one will hear your message if you're a messy bitch. No matter which cause you take up or how you choose to fight for it, you need to lay the groundwork before you let someone catch those magical hands. (Metaphorically speaking, of course. Violence is the epitome of counterproductive.)

## Quick Refresher

You've come a long fucking way from the first pages of this book, so you might need a little refresher on how to prep for magical activism.

- Meditate on what you can do
- Take small, achievable steps
- Play to your strengths
- Give everyone a job
- Be flexible (always have a plan and a backup plan)

- Practice with your sisters
- Take good fucking care of yourself

And maybe most importantly, make sure you have your shit together—physically, mentally, emotionally, *and* magically—before you go charging into any battles.

---

# Channel Some Clarity into Your Message

A lot of fighting for a cause is convincing other people to care about it. To do that, you have to have a clear intent and an even clearer message. Ask yourself all the questions: Who does the problem affect? Who can effect the most change? What are your long-term goals? What do you hope will happen? (This is the time to dream big, witches!) The best way to motivate people is to let them know exactly what you want them to do. And when you're clear on that yourself, you'll naturally infuse your communications with that intention.

### ✦ Don't Get in Your Own F*cking Way

Once you get clear on your message, make sure nothing detracts from it—not your appearance, word choice, or attitude. The work might not be glamorous, but you need to bring your all to it in order for your magic to take hold. You want people to walk away with your message and know exactly what their next steps are. Be confident but not argumentative (and definitely not a condescending dick). The goal here is to empower people, not embarrass them or piss them off. One way to do that is to tell a story. Just remember to adjust your message to the medium you're using. No one wants to read a thread that's thirty Tweets deep.

### ✦ Know Your Sh*t Backward and Forward

When you're getting the word out about your cause, you need to be able to answer any question and counter any argument. If studying was never your strong suit, try witching up your next session. Hold onto a fluorite crystal—which can help with clarity, focus, intellect, and memory—and meditate for a few minutes before you dig in. See yourself passionately and convincingly rattling off facts like a fucking expert, and feel the other person receiving the information in a positive way. Then get down to business. You should find that you're able to concentrate and retain information better than before.

## PRACTICAL MAGIC

There are two kinds of spells: the kind that uses supplies, and the kind that uses you (your whole self, mind and body). The second kind includes "embodying your spell," which means acting your desired reality into being over an hour, day, week, month, year, or lifetime. For at least a few minutes a day, feel yourself living the life you want to live in the kind of world you hope to create. Put another way, you fake it 'til you make it. You have to make it believable. When you do, your energy will work overtime to bring it into being.

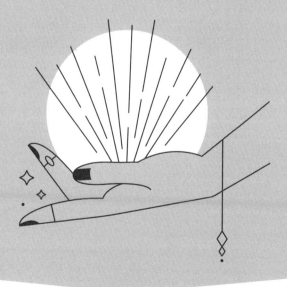

# Put Your Energy Where It Counts

Magic is limitless. Human beings are not. So think of yourself like a character in a video game with an energy meter, and make sure you don't deplete your energy on stupid shit. You have to strike a balance between strategy and action. Do a little strategizing and decide where your energy is best spent *before* you spend it. You also need to learn how to recognize a lost cause when you see it. Don't dig in your heels because you're already invested. Take what's left of your energy wherever it'll do the most good.

### ✦ Do Your F*cking Research

This is not the time to throw shit at the wall and see what sticks. By doing a little power mapping and targeting the people who can effect the most change, you can be more effective with your energy. Meditate on your cause and see the people in its direct orbit. Keep in mind that the most effective person may not be the most powerful—a CEO might rely on their assistant to triage a lot of their work, making the assistant the person to reach out to. And a politician up for reelection might be more persuadable than a CEO. Take some time to look into the possibilities you come up with and think of how you can apply your talents to reaching them.

### ✦ Use the Coven to Your Advantage

This is another time where playing to your strengths and leapfrogging over your weaknesses can be a winning strategy. If one of your sisters is better at writing and another loves public speaking, then assignments should absolutely be handed out accordingly. If one witch gets hot-headed and another can keep her cool, the chill one should be out front. Unless you're desperate, you should never force a witch into a situation that makes her truly uncomfortable. It'll hinder her magic and render her pretty ineffectual, which is the opposite of what you're going for here.

### ✦ Know When to Walk Away

Energy is everything—don't waste it on people who won't fucking listen. When you realize that someone's not going to budge, be like badass congresswoman

## CRYSTAL F*CKING CLEAR

If you're a little anxious about the actual activism, crystals can help. All you need is a little insurance. Aquamarine, for instance, can clear the Throat Chakra and boost your confidence. Turquoise can turn you into a smooth talker. And when you need a way to condense how you feel into cohesive sentences, lapis lazuli can help you tap into your truth. There are plenty of other stones that can act as a magical safety net for this part of your journey. Just do a quick search for whatever it is you hope to amplify.

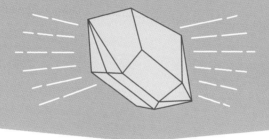

Maxine Waters and reclaim your damn time. In other words, walk away. Your energy is worth more than the effort it would take to convince some people who are determined to remain ignorant or unhelpful. The trick is knowing when that's the case, because it's not always obvious (especially when dealing with professional politicians who know how to placate concerned constituents). Use your witchy intuition to know who's being real and who's wasting your time.

## Follow Up

Asking people to hear you out and care about what you care about is a lot like interviewing for a job. And although it's a dying art, the post-interview thank you is still super important. You don't need to break out the fancy stationery (although it probably couldn't hurt, and you *could* bless it before sending it). Just politely thank people for their time. But make sure you also sum up your point and make it easy for the person to act. Staying on message from hello to goodbye keeps your energy (and its recipient) focused.

## WITCH, YOU GOT THIS!

The first thing you have to do is get clear on what you want from people. Your message is the most important part of your magical activism, so it's worth spending some time on getting it right and targeting the people who need to hear it most.

Set your intention (your message)
Tell people what you want them to do
Don't trip over your own ego or anger
Study the issue
Don't waste your energy or time
Play to your strengths
Always follow up

From beginning to end, understanding and communicating the action you want others to take imbues your work with your intention, making every interaction more powerful.

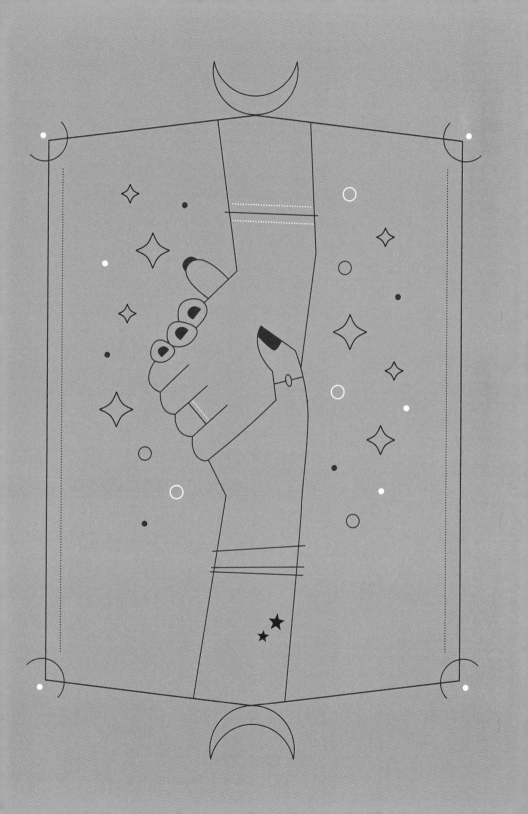

"Women are the real architects of society."

— ( • ) —

# CHAPTER 15

# GET. SH*T. DONE.

There is nothing a group of strong, like-minded women cannot accomplish. Sure, a small coven might not be able to stop climate change or racism in its tracks. But it can engage a community, change the minds of politicians, and advocate for the people affected. It's time to take that kickass energy to the streets. You'll be amazed at what you can accomplish by combining old-school magical principles with modern-day methods of fighting for justice, tolerance, and change.

## Cast a Spell

The written word is pretty damn powerful even before you add magic to the mix. With a few energetic tweaks, you can put a spell on your readers. (But not literally, because that would be ethically tricky stuff.) You can, however, inspire them to action like never before. Start by tapping into your intuition, letting the message come to you and flow through you. Think of your target audience and what would move them while you write, being sure to observe the rules of polite communication even when you're really pissed off. And then infuse your message with a little something witchy just to seal the deal.

### ✦ Start with Common Sense

When writing to people who can help you create the change you want to see, you definitely want your passion for the cause to shine through. You don't want your purpose to get lost in flowery language, angry criticisms, or a long-ass story. And remember that all the magic in the world can't help you if you piss off the person you're asking for help. Positive, polite letters are going to be way more fucking effective than mean Tweets. Keep your words clear and your sentences simple while adding just enough personal story to highlight the importance of the issue to real people. And make sure you end with an easy action the reader can take.

### ✦ Add a Magical Touch

There are a ton of ways to give your message a magical boost. The easiest of these is to infuse it with your intention. Hold your intention in your mind before you start writing, and feel it flowing through your fingers as you type. If you're submitting a physical letter, you can bless the paper, use "magical ink" (sold

## PRACTICAL MAGIC

Hermes isn't the only god who can back you up while you work your activist magic. With a pantheon of gods available to you, not to mention your ancestors and other spirits, you can find help for pretty much any cause. For general aid, send an offering to Athena, the goddess of wisdom and political strategy. For more specific subjects, do a quick search. If you want help fighting on behalf of nature, for example, you could call on Demeter. Hell, you could even call in the big gun—Gaia. She'd probably be down to help you get some protective legislation passed. Just make sure you're searching for an appropriate offering while you search for appropriate deities. They don't work for free.

online), and even add a sigil beneath your signature or over the seal of the envelope. Whether your message is physical or virtual, you can call on Hermes, god of communication, to ensure the message reaches its destination and is read and absorbed. (You could use an old-timey prayer for this. But if any deity keeps up with modern messaging, Hermes definitely does. Have you seen his kicks?

# Talk the Talk

If you're a charming public speaker and a lively conversationalist, use it to your fucking advantage. Fill your words with your intention, infusing each one with world-changing energy. Hit up social media and make videos showing people why they should care about shit and how they can help. Make sure every communication includes a CTA (call to action). Not everyone will make the connection between what you're saying and what they should be doing about it. You have to make it as easy and enchanting as possible for them. On a magical note: make sure you ground yourself before speaking so that what comes out is clear and centered.

### ✦ Go Viral (Or Try To)

If you're a social-media guru, now's your time to shine! Get out the word on every platform, and make sure you're sharing important information from other activists and important figures in the field. Explainers and behind-the-scenes videos can be incredibly helpful in getting people engaged. Even if your following is small, encourage friends to like and share your work. And don't underestimate the power of (respectfully) calling people out on social media. Sometimes, that's just how shit gets done. You may be just a drop in the virtual ocean, but you never know how far those ripples will travel.

### ✦ Just F*cking Talk to People

Don't just be an armchair activist, though—use that energy IRL. The idea of talking to strangers may be a completely foreign one these days, but it's still effective. Knocking on doors is a great way to shore up support. Of course, it's best if you do it as part of an organization that's vetted who's on the other side of those doors. But word of mouth can be just as effective in other ways. You can make phone calls and/or organize a call-in campaign. You can also let friends know how to make an impact, especially if they live in an area with a vested interest or an impending election. If you get nervous, hold a communication-friendly or courage-instilling stone in your palm. Confidence gets shit done, so do what you gotta do to feel empowered.

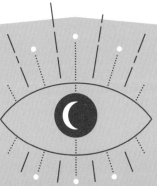

## KNOW YOUR SH'T ABOUT SAFETY

Unfortunately, activism has a long history of being a risky endeavor. The safety of yourself and your coven should be your number-one priority. Don't engage with crazy. And you don't want to bring glass spell jars or charms, which could break and cut you if you get shoved around. But there's no harm in asking your spirits (family, friends, former activists, gods) to have your back. Either way, be extra vigilant when you're in a potentially dangerous situation. Turn on your magical Spidey sense and feel the energy of the space. If you feel it shift negatively, get the fuck out of there. And if you're coming from a place of privilege, be prepared to put yourself in front of anyone in your group who doesn't share that privilege. Yours gives you an advantage they don't have.

## Walk the Walk

Nothing gets done if you don't take action. Don't just talk about the shit you want to do to change the world. Get out there and start fucking doing it. Take one tiny step each day and watch your efforts snowball. Radiate powerful energy into your every effort. From working spells and making calls at home to doing community outreach and exercising your right to vote, you can change the world in so many powerful ways. You don't have to be Greta Thunberg to start a small, sustainable community garden and provide families with fresh food. But if you want to join Greta on her press tours, you can work toward that, too. Set your intention like she sets the sails on her zero-emissions boats, and you can do anything you put your fucking mind to.

### WITCH, YOU GOT THIS!

You did it! You are a fully fledged badass magical activist
who's ready to tackle the big issues head-on.
It's time to put all that hard work to good use.

Harness the power of the written word
Catch more bees with honey
Add a magical boost to your efforts
Tweet like your life depends on it
Knock on some doors
Protect your personal safety
Create change. Every. Damn. Day.

You've got your girls. You're up on all the magic. Your coven is a well-oiled machine. You're ready to take everything you've learned and change the world with it. So what's stopping you? Not a damn thing.

# MAGICAL BATTERY- RECHARGING RITUAL

Magical activism is fucking amazing, but it can also be a lot. Between working spells and physically pounding the pavement to get shit done, it's not uncommon to suddenly find your low-battery light flashing.

This ritual uses amplifiers of calm, self-love, and clarity to wash away all the energetic bullshit that's weighing you down. It's not a replacement for some serious self-care and a full charge, but it can give you a little boost when you need it most.

## MAGICAL MATERIALS

Bowl of warm water

Lavender essential oil

White candles

Dried lavender

One or two rose petals

Rose quartz crystal(s)

Clear quartz crystal(s)

### CLEVER WITCH TIP

Don't let your battery get *too* low before performing a ritual like this. There's only so much it can do if you're running on empty.

## 1: Start with Your Intention

You can go one of two ways with your intention: Ask to be replenished, or affirm to yourself that you are more than enough. Which you choose depends on what's making you feel drained. Is it physical exhaustion? Or is it something closer to imposter syndrome? The ritual is the same either way, but the intention can make all the difference in how you feel afterward.

## 2: Take a Breath

Place your bowl of water in front of you and, holding onto your intention, add a few drops of soothing lavender essential oil. Take the deepest breath you've taken all day, letting the smell of lavender fill you with calm.

## 3: Dress Up Your Ritual

Light at least one candle, not only to amplify your intention but also to bring in those self-care vibes. (You can anoint it with the lavender oil, too, if you feel like it.) Crush the lavender in your hands and sprinkle it onto the surface of the water, then drop the rose petals on top of it. Finally, place the crystals around the bowl, for good fucking measure. Feel your little self-care setup attracting an energy of love and light.

## 4: Use Your Hands

Place one hand, palm down, over the water and the other, palm up, facing the sky. Bring your intention to mind again and feel the positive energy around you flowing into your skyward hand, recharging your battery. Let it flow through your body and into the water via your other hand.

## 5: Plug In

Now infused with the powerful positive energy of the Universe and the loving properties of your magical materials, the water is ready for you to use. Slip your hands into it and lovingly wash them while the water's energy fills you up. See it starting at your fingertips and slowly spreading up your arms, through your heart, up to your head and down to your toes. See yourself radiant and recharged.

### MAGICAL MOD

When you're really fucking worn out, turn this tabletop hand-washing ritual into a full-body soak. Set everything up the same way, using the bathtub as your bowl of water. Go even bigger on the lavender and rose petals for a luxurious spa-like experience. When the water is ready, slip your whole body into it and feel the water's energy enveloping you like a warm hug from your favorite person. Then just enjoy the hell out of some much-deserved me-time!

# INDEX